GOLD IN YOUR MEMORIES

GOLD IN YOUR MEMORIES

Sacred Moments, Glimpses of God

MACRINA WIEDERKEHR, O.S.B.

AVE MARIA PRESS Notre Dame, Indiana 46556

Library of Congress Cataloging-in-Publication Data

Wiederkehr, Macrina.
        Gold in your memories : sacred moments, glimpses of God / Macrina
Wiederkehr.
            p.   cm.
        Includes bibliographical references.
        ISBN 0-87793-665-X (hardcover). — ISBN 0-87793-664-1 (pbk.)
        1. Spirituality—Catholic Church.   2. Memory—Religious aspects—Chris-
tianity.   I. Title.
BX2350.65.W54   1998
248.4'6—dc21   98-27037
        CIP

For my family.

In loving memory of
my parents
Henry Güller Wiederkehr
Marion Smith Ferguson Eveld
and my sister
Dorothy Alice.

For my sisters and brothers
Ann, Ray, Joe,
Edna, Basil, Mary Lou
and
my nieces and nephews.

You are all gold in my memories.

Acknowledgments

I am grateful to those who have shared in the birthing of *Gold in Your Memories*:

Julianne Christine Brooks, Elaine Magruder, Shaun McCarty, Don Streit, Judith Weaver, and Ann Young who read all or portions of this work and offered me affirmation and supportive suggestions for improvement;

Catherine Markey and JoAnn Senko who gifted me with generous portions of their time in careful proofreading;

Eugene and Sandra Scherm whose lake house in Hot Springs, Arkansas, became a hermitage for me as I began this book;

Victor and Jo Betsy Szebehely who offered me writing space on Penobscot Bay as this work neared completion, and Paula D'Arcy and Joyce Rupp who shared that space and *remembered* with me;

Frank Cunningham and Bob Hamma at Ave Maria Press. The warm welcome and encouragement I have received in this new publishing relationship is deeply appreciated.

Introduction

The Gold in Your Memories

A Mosaic of Memories

Memories of Books I Have Loved

Finding Your Way to the Gold: The Path of Ritual

Conclusion

Food for the Soul: An Offering of Books

INTRODUCTION

Such good things can happen
to people who learn to remember!

—Emily Dickinson

Today many people are finding ways to remember. They are integrating into their lives lost and forgotten memories. They are carefully putting their souls and bodies back together again. They are re-membering. This is essential life-work: re-shaping, re-fashioning, re-calling. It is the work of an artist. We are all artists and creators of our own lives if we can but put ourselves into the heart of the Great Artist and *remember*.

It has not escaped my attention that when people are drawn into working with memories these days there is an excessive concentration on the painful memories. To some extent this is perhaps understandable and even necessary for a while because there is much healing that needs to take place in so many lives. It is not only that our memories need to be healed. It seems more accurate to say they need to be received, accepted, and integrated into our lives so that healing can take place.

I sometimes think we are a little overly zealous in our efforts to become whole. I don't know that we will ever be whole. I believe that God calls us to be *in process* and this means one step at a time, one minute at a time, one day at a time. A faithfulness to living our lives *in process* is, perhaps, even more important than all our efforts to become whole.

This book is a gathering of memories. Just as you might gather around the fireplace in little family circles, looking through old photo albums, I am inviting you to gather the memories of the ages into your consciousness. This will be a homecoming.

Since all of your memories are invited we can be fairly certain that some of the painful ones will show up. Memories don't necessarily come in order and they don't arrive in exclusive groups labeled, "Joyful Memories Only!" "Painful Memories Only!" They come to us all mixed up. In fact, one of the wondrously helpful discoveries in my life has been that it is quite possible to be happy and sad all in the same moment.

Thus, as you begin to gather your memories you will recall moments of feeling gloriously alive, renewed, full of hope, and fulfilled; and you will probably also remember times of despair when you felt nothing but loneliness, misunderstanding, neglect, or rejection. There will be memories of great loss, feelings of failure, sadness, fear, and confusion just as there will be memories of success and victory, memories of being loved and in love, moments of great joy and a sense of peace. You will remember moments of exquisite beauty and wonder, and you may also recall what seemed like decades during which all loveliness was hidden from you.]

Perhaps there will be the memory of times when you were not treated with honor and respect, even memories of abuse. Alongside those painful memories you will recall the loving people who were there to help restore your hope. There were those who stood beside you, enabling you to discover your own goodness and worth as you pieced your life back together. The memory of your remarkable resilience, your ability to forgive and to heal may be a special comfort to you.

I am convinced that our joyful memories have often been overlooked, like some undiscovered gold. I am making a special effort to help you call those memories into your consciousness, for I suspect we have not fully realized their potential and their place in our healing work. This is a book about the gold in your memories.]

How can you remember the gold so it can continue to bless you today? First of all, you will have to acknowledge its presence in your life. It is difficult to search for something you don't believe in. Secondly, you will need to spend a lot of time with your soul. The soul thrives on remembering. Feed it memories and it comes alive. And it will help you to recall more memories if you show even the slightest interest in remembering.

There is a way that the soul can get crowded out of one's day. The soul is a bit shy and does not demand center stage. She lives a life of her own, and yet there are soulprints in every fiber of your being, even in the things you've forgotten. The soul is the keeper of memories. She knows where beauty is stored. She contains the memories of your entire life. Deep in your unconscious she stands guard. If you are in need of a particular memory she can reveal it to you and help you to bear both the beauty and the pain. She knows all about the gold in your memories.

She remembers the dewdrop you tried to pick up when you were only four years old; it glistened in the sunshine and you thought it was a bright, colored marble. She remembers the bird that flew into the windshield and died when you were ten years old and how you cried all the way home. She can still see you on those cold winter evenings, huddled about the fire telling stories and making up silly songs. She remembers the candles you lit for your sister to make up for losing her locket, and the many times you wanted to say you were sorry but didn't know how.

The soul remembers all the sunrises and sunsets you've ever seen. She can tell you where you were, what you were wearing, and what kind of mood you were in. She remembers the sunset in Ogalala, Nebraska, and the peace that came from sharing it with a good friend. She remembers you pouring your heart out to another friend long ago on top of a haystack in the prairies of South Dakota.

She knows about all the yearnings of your heart, your moments of loneliness, your struggle to be in life-giving relationships. And she remembers that summer in Texas when you met your best friend.

She remembers every path you've taken in your search for God. She knows all of the seasons when God seemed absent in your life. She remembers those evenings when you used to sit by the lake waiting for Jesus to come walking across the waters. She can still see the times when you opened yourself up completely to God's presence. She was there at your birth. She will be there at your death when she enters fully into the heart of God and into the hearts of those you have loved while on this earth.

Although I'm describing the soul as an intimate companion, if we have not yet discovered the gold in our lives, we may have lived all these years without a consciousness of the soul's presence. So what do we mean when we say that someone is living "without soul"? Perhaps we are suggesting that such a person has not learned how to let the painful memories work for their good. Maybe they have chosen to remain a victim of the past, never having experienced the process of integration. They've not discovered the gold. To live in this way is, indeed, to live without soul.

So give the soul a chance, a chance to help you mine your golden memories. Take some time for solitude and ask yourself this question: What is the gold in my memories? Listen deeply and perhaps write your response to that question in your journal.

Since I'm asking you about the gold in your memories, I've searched my soul to see what my own golden memories might be. Although there are many, I've singled out just a few to share with you.

Some of my most wonderful memories are of the early morning hours. I love morning. When people say to me, "I'm just not a morning person," I always suggest they try morning for seven days, just to see what happens. Of course the talent lies in being able to determine just when morning will need to begin for you. If there are children in your household, you might have to get up ahead of them, before they are trying to find the partners to their socks, quarreling about who is staying in the bathroom too long or whose turn it is to get the prize in the cereal box.

I remember a morning in Galveston when the sun pushed through the stars with such reverence that I could barely tell when the night ended and the day began. And as the sun was rising, on that same morning, I broke bread with friends and we celebrated the joys and sorrows of our lives. It was "a paschal-mystery" moment, a sharing in the dying and rising of Jesus. The silhouettes of the fishermen off in the distance reminded me of Jesus having breakfast with his friends on the beach.

There are memories of mornings from my childhood when the mockingbird seemed to be singing the sun right out of the night. There is one particular morning from my teenage years when the song of the cardinal in the mulberry tree, the spectacular colors of the sunrise, and the dewy freshness of the morning worked an incredible healing in my life.

There is a memory of a cloudy morning in Oregon. A light mist was falling. It was very early. I was sitting on a bench overlooking the Willamette River, and the lights of the city were faintly glimmering through the vapor rising from the waters below, creating a mystical scene. Although, at that moment, my life felt quite tattered by concerns, decisions, and trying to figure out how to grow up, that morning is still a gift, still present in my soul.

Morning is one of my life's symbols. It always seems to work for my good when I spend time in it. It is the hour of the day when my soul gets excited in a quiet sort of way. Nothing spectacular needs to be going on. I may be taking a walk on our monastery grounds, or watching the turtles stick their heads out of the pond, or making coffee for my sisters. Morning is definitely part of the gold in my memories.

We live our lives in the spaces between all those memories. And the spaces in between give us opportunities to make new memories. Memories matter. They are a part of who we are. In writing a book about memories I am not suggesting that we live our lives in the past, only that we claim all the pieces. They are, as one poet suggests, like beads of life gathered together to create a beautiful "necklace of experience."

As I lead you on your own pilgrimage of memory, I offer you Nancy Wood's poem "The Beads of Life" for an opening prayer.

> The space between events is where
> most of life is lived. Those half-remembered moments
> of joy or sadness, fear or disappointment, are merely
> beads of life strung together
> to make one expanding necklace of experience.
>
> The space between events is where
> we grow old. From sunrise to sunset one day lives
> as another day emerges from the fluid womb of dawn,

the first bead strung upon
the everlasting thread of life.

The space between events is where
knowledge marries beauty. In quiet reflection
we remember only the colored outline of events,
the black and white of war, the rosiness
that surrounded our first love.

The space between events is why
we go on living. The laughter of a child or
the sigh of wind in a canyon becomes the music
we hear expanding in our hearts each time
we gather one more bead of life.[1]

THE GOLD IN YOUR MEMORIES

. . . there is a place deep inside
where one's real life goes on,
much like an underground river
in parched, dry country,
which flows
whether one knows about it or not.

—Sharon Butala
The Perfection of the Morning

It was a mild February afternoon in the hill country of Texas. A few gold leaves had lasted through the winter ice storms of the Frio Canyon where I sat above the river. I was waiting for whatever one waits for when the ghost of a book suddenly pushes its face above the waters whispering, "Write me!"

I had been nurturing a desire to write a book on memories for a long time and I was, perhaps, being overly cautious. After all, I consider myself a person with an eye for finding grace in the present moment and I have attempted to lead others on that path as well. I know something of the harm that can come from trying to live in memory lane.

But a memory kept rising of a little girl lying in a coffin whose face I'd almost forgotten. A voice rose up in some unattended part of my soul saying ever so softly, *"There is gold in your memories."* At that moment a tiny gold leaf slipped from a wintered bush beside me and floated dreamily down into the green Frio River. "Yes," the river seemed to echo, "There is gold in your memories." Wait! I protested. I know a lot of people who would look me straight in the eye and say, "There is no gold in my memories!"

"Ah," the voice continued, "if such is the case, will it not be a joy to enable them to see that they themselves are the gold that has come through those memories?"

Our life experiences are our best teachers. Hidden in our sometimes painful history are lessons waiting to be learned. We are taught not only by life's harsh events; beautiful and comforting experiences also contain seeds of wisdom that reappear in our time of need. We can return to these remembrances and let them continue to be for us a school of life. We learn lessons from both the pain and the joy. In the underground river of our unconscious all of these memories wait for us.

If the memory is painful, it may stay out of sight until you are ready to receive it. It waits until you are able to befriend it. Then it will rise to the surface to be integrated into your life. It will become one of your teachers.

If your heart is broken, torn open by memories of things that never should have been, there will come a time when you must take hold of your own hand and learn of the courage that lives deep in the sea of your unconscious. There a sweet strength waits to hold you, to cup your face and turn it toward the sunlight after a long winter of hibernation. Hibernation is not the same as hiding. Occasionally you need a time of hibernation. You hibernate until you grow strong and wise enough to lean into your painful stories, allowing them to harmonize with your life. While embracing these life stories, you learn to let spring take hold of you again and show you the flowers you've forgotten.

The "flowers" are people, experiences, and moments you once held dear. They have been places of healing for you. There is a deep reservoir of beautiful memories within the human soul. These are all part of the gold in your storehouse of memories. There are times when it can be healthy to return to these moments, allowing them to be a kind of massage for the soul's aches. In your spirit you can be there in that sacred place, with some loving person, in a moment of gladness, or with a certain piece of beauty. You can touch again that moment and distill grace and comfort from it because it is part of your history. Every year of your life, all the ages you have ever been rest in you as part of your heritage. We are like those brightly painted Russian nesting dolls. Open one doll and you find the surprise of another tucked away inside. Each doll can represent a particular phase of life.

REMEMBERING BEAUTY

Each season of life contains unique memories. Sometimes our painful memories take center stage and force the golden memories to retreat. Certain seasons of my childhood, for example, were lived in terror that we were going to lose our farm. For some reason I recall being especially fearful in the spring. Perhaps it was because everything was so lush and beautiful at that time, and it broke my heart to think of losing it or having to move away to some unknown land. Or maybe it was because this was the season when my family depended on the earth's elements to work in our favor so that the grape harvest would be good. Would there be too little rain or too much? Would destructive storms damage the crops? Sometimes I would hear my parents quarreling or worrying together about the future. This was a very unpleasant fear, and it would often surface mightily in my young heart. It was a fear I could never talk about with my parents, since I thought that talking about it might make it happen or add pain to my already-worried parents.

Alongside the memory of that fear lives another memory. It is the memory of buttercups. Although there were many meadows of wildflowers on our family farm in the spring and summer, my favorite was nestled in the northwest corner on the edge of the forest. At the entrance of the forest, thick carpets of green moss flourished. Mingled in with the bright green moss and extending into the north meadow, buttercups grew in abundance.

That field of buttercups was the lap of God for me. It was a meadow of hospitality, a sanctuary for my fears. It was like going to a parent for comfort. I felt at peace there. It was as though some kind of holy energy oozed out of the ground and filled me with God. As a child, I would never have used this kind of descriptive language to explain what was going on, but these are the thoughts that come to me today. I find myself looking back at that meadow and asking just what was going on there. What special grace did I experience while sitting in my field of buttercups?

I am beginning to perceive a divine energy that exudes from the earth. Could it be the energy of the first day of creation? Or is it perhaps what, in the Catholic tradition, we call sanctifying grace? Whatever we name it, I sense that it is accessible at every moment. In that field of buttercups, because of my vulnerability and openness, I was being blessed and immersed in God's life.

I was being healed by beauty. When I think back to my meadow-moments, it is the beauty I remember most clearly. Perhaps beauty is God's memory of the Divine, made visible.

God is remembering herself. God is remembering himself. Beauty has medicinal qualities, and we would do well to reflect more carefully upon this truth in regard to healing. I am beginning to realize now, in my adult life, those buttercups have not gone away. They are still accessible. When I am in need of a healing memory I sometimes invite them on to my path again. Is there anything you have stored away that might be valuable in companioning you in some of your life's dark moments?

One evening during shared prayer I asked a circle of my sisters to try to remember a moment of beauty in which they had experienced healing. The result was enriching. Almost without thinking, each sister spontaneously shared a memory of being touched and renewed by some aspect of nature.

Gertie was reminded of a moment of sadness. She was feeling very much alone and found herself outside walking as if on some unknown quest. Mysteriously she was drawn to a tree. As she stood gazing at that tree a presence seemed to replace her sadness. She walked closer and found herself leaning against the tree. Bonding with it as a friend, the tree became a sacred presence, a mentor, a guide.

Audrey spoke of standing in awe before Niagara Falls. Listening to its phenomenal melody was like being at a symphony. In those rushing waters she sensed an incredible power and was drawn to wonder about the Source. The water cascading out and falling into the river below was an experience of grace. That memory is one to which she can return. It is like music for her soul, a baptism of beauty.

Stephanie shared a memory of when she was a young sister in formation. It was her first home-visit after a tough novitiate. Her brother, who was also in monastic life, was with her. One night they decided to go frog-gigging. It was a full moon night. When they got to the pond, there was the moon, hauntingly lovely, shimmering in the water. They sat down on the bank, began talking, enjoying the radiance of the full moon along with all the unique night sounds that those who live in the country experience. So deep into soul-sharing they went that their intention of frog-gigging was quite forgotten (lucky frogs!). Suddenly they were astounded to discover it was two o'clock in the morning. In the beauty of the night and the friendship of sister and brother sharing, they had lost all sense of time.

Rosalie's memory was that of driving home one evening. The sky had a blue-gray stormy appearance, although the sun kept faintly breaking through the clouds. She was listening to Strauss's waltz on the radio and feeling as if she were part of the music and the sky. Suddenly into that already mystical sky a flock of geese appeared, flying in two layers. They did not seem to be flying in formation, but rather moving slowly to the Strauss waltz. The moment was uplifting and unforgettable.

My memory was one of hiking in the Rockies with a friend. It was September and the Aspen season was at its peak. Suddenly along the trail to my right I came upon a small tree growing out of a rocky cliff. A tiny golden leaf hung on one of its branches. All the other leaves were gone. The coal black bluff behind the tree served as an exquisite backdrop for the golden leaf. It was a striking image and I thought how I would have missed the beauty of that one solitary leaf if the little tree had been filled with many leaves. There was a unique beauty in its being there in solitude—all alone. I've never forgotten that leaf. Although I have a picture of it that I treasure, I don't really need that picture. The original image remains in my soul.

Each of these colorful scenes is like walking through the soul's art gallery. At any moment we can call up a piece of beauty or a loving memory from those deep places in our spirits. For there is within each of us a magical place where the original breath of life abides. That sacred place within us cannot be destroyed. No matter how intense the pain in our lives may have been, there is a life that waits to renew us and be received by us again.

Awakening Beauty

The stories I have shared are reminders that remembering beauty can be a healing ointment, capable of soothing the wounds of the ages. Once there was a man who was restored to life through his remembrance of beauty. Some of you have met this man in the children's classic *The Secret Garden*. When Lord Craven's wife died, he locked himself in the walled fortress of his pain. In a sense he died with her, refusing to receive life from anyone including his young son, Colin. Nothing seemed strong enough or soft enough to break the walls of his self-made prison. One day, however, the magic that waits in each of us found him slightly open. The passage about his awakening is worth our reflection as we consider the gold of our own memories.

> He sat and gazed at the sunlit water and his eyes began to see things growing at its edge. There was one lovely mass of blue forget-me-nots growing so close to the stream that its leaves were wet and at these he found himself looking as he remembered he had looked at such things years ago. He was actually thinking tenderly how lovely it was and what wonders of blue its hundreds of little blossoms were. He did not know that just that simple thought was slowly filling his mind—filling and filling it until other things were softly pushed aside. It was as if a sweet clear spring had begun to rise in a stagnant pool and had risen and risen until at last it swept the dark water away . . . the valley seemed to grow quieter and quieter as he stared at the bright delicate blueness . . . at last he moved as if he were awakening and he got up slowly and stood on the moss carpet, drawing a long, deep, soft breath. . . . Something seemed to have been unbound and released in him, very quietly.
>
> "What is it?" he said, almost in a whisper, and he passed his hand over his forehead. "I almost feel as if I were alive."[1]

Lord Craven was experiencing one of those golden memories stored away in his soul. The forget-me-nots served as a symbol. They helped him get in touch with the joy that was being kept safe for him. When he discovered that he was still capable of deep feeling, the soft things were able to return and soothe his tired spirit. The magical place had not dried up. The prison walls were beginning to crumble all because he was allowing himself to experience the beautiful again.

> A thing of beauty is a joy forever;
> Its loveliness increases; It will never
> Pass into nothingness.[2]

We are fortunate that the world is still full of poets who remind us of this truth. You, too, have within you the memory of a thing of beauty that will endure forever. If you call out to it, it will return.

Can you remember moments when joy came back to you after a long absence? Do you believe that even during stormy times when all seems dark and foreboding, there is a place of calm within you? Are you aware that there is a life in you that no one can destroy? Can you accept the truth that within you *a thing of beauty* is being kept safe for you? What is it that needs to be awakened or restored in you? What are some ways you might access life's golden moments, joyful memories from the past that have grown dim? Is there anything you would like to retrieve from your soul's storehouse? What is the gold in your memories?

FRAMING YOUR MEMORIES

To assist you in reflecting more deeply on ways to access those things of beauty hidden in you, I'm offering you a jewel of a way that has worked for me. One day while I was doing a piece of healing work I remembered a tiny poem, the Japanese haiku, that one of my teachers taught me to write. A haiku is a three-line poem with a syllable pattern of five, seven, five. Some haiku are written in four lines. The important thing to remember is that the first and last line each has five syllables. All the words in between, whether written as one or two lines, contain seven syllables.

Frederick Buechner describes the haiku as a way of putting a frame around an experience.[3] I like that very much.

Whether you are writing a haiku about a past or present event, you stand still and enter into the experience. This is a way of immortalizing a moment in time. The question to ask as you write your haiku is: What do I see and how can I express what I see without cluttering up my vision with words? Indeed, writing your haiku is painting a picture with only a few words. For those of us who love words this may prove to be quite a sacrifice. We are being asked to let go of words. We strive to be faithful to the experience, to be present with the lens of the eye.

In creating your haiku, strive to say what you see in the simplest way possible, whether what you need to say is delightful or painful. Perhaps underneath the pain you will discover a certain gift unnoticed until now. You may come to understand how the courage, love, and wisdom you possess today grew out of that painful life experience.

As you begin the process of getting in touch with those things of beauty hidden from your sight, find a comfortable place where you are least likely to be disturbed. Look into your life as though you were watching home movies. Take one particular event and try to get it in focus. Put a frame around this experience as though it were a piece of art. It is! It's a piece of your life! You are a work of art. The Divine Artist is standing nearby trying to help you reverence the shades and colors of your life. As the curtain is drawn up on one of your life's memories be prayerfully present at the scene. Just receive it without making any judgment about it.

If it is a joyful memory it will be easy to let the curtain rise. It might, however, be a memory of pain, rejection, sadness, loss, or sin. Capturing such a moment in a little poem somehow puts a seal on it. It's a way of claiming it as a part of your life and as one of your teachers. Everything on your path can be a guide for you unless you send it away.

I am sharing with you a few haiku that I have written in various seasons of my life. You will notice that on occasion I have diverted from the given syllable pattern of five, seven, five. When I'm in the classroom of life rather than an academic classroom I always feel free to break a few rules. The goal here is to be faithful to your inner vision.

Look at each of these haiku as a painting drawn with words. Are you able to see the pictures?

A tiny gold leaf
offers a silent sermon
from a barren branch.

Fear is in my heart
the buttercups console me
in my healing field.

Two friends journeying
through the forest at midnight
to visit the moon.

After the hail storm
Papa looks toward the vineyards
my heart breaks with love.

My first memory of snow
Oh so much sugar, I thought
falling from heaven.

Sleeping outside on a summer night
I pull a blanket of stars over me
and listen to the whippoorwill.

The tiger lily
stretching toward
the morning sun
drinks in the dew drops.

Casting aside fear
like wildflowers on the hillside
I abide in love.

The red tennis shoes
left out in the rain last night
are filled with rain water.

Longing for warmth
I hasten to the kitchen
on cold winter mornings.

In the dark of night
the stars fall into the lake
until morning comes.

Observe how each of these little poems creates a visual image of a memory from my past. In most cases you were probably able to visualize the scene. Although some of these memories evoke feelings of sadness, I am usually able to glean something positive from this exercise of remembering.

To reach into your memories and mine the gold is not always an easy task. This requires prayerful reflection and practice. It is worth all your effort, though, as you look into the mirror of life one day and know, without a doubt, that *you are the gold* who has come through all those memories.

When you can do this you will be on your way to becoming an integrated person. You have chosen not to remain a victim. You have looked your life straight in the eye, held out your hand, and said, "You are mine; I will walk with you!" At the end of this chapter, as part of your writing exercise, I will ask you to create haiku in which you paint a picture of the gold in your memories. In preparation for this exercise, then, I am asking you one more time:

What is the gold in your memories?

Have you explored the attics and basements of your life to see if some priceless nuggets are hidden there? The gold is that which is able to soften your heart and restore your hope. It is the discovery of an incredible courage, integrity, and faith that has endured through the storms of your life. It may also be the memory of loving people who have stood beside you, or beautiful moments that have comforted you. It can especially be the memory of beauty.

Beauty is a wordless sermon on the mystery of the Divine Presence in our world. The appearance of beauty and our ability to receive it is a revelation of God in our lives. Beauty is one of the faces of God. It is God's memory of all that is holy and good, faithful and true. It often appears upon the scene when hope seems gone. It has the power to heal, restore, comfort, and delight that part of you that is overcome with grief. Beauty is God's way of reminding you of your own beauty. It is God remembering you.

The poet William Blake suggests that there is a moment in everyone's day that the demons cannot find. In other words, there is a place in the depths of your being that is protected and saved for you. It is an inner space, guarded by God's presence. There in that sacred place no harm can reach you. To arrive at that special place, however, you sometimes have to journey through a frightening forest of dark shadows with many obstacles along the way. The land of the dark forest is not a place to settle into and call home. Nor, however, is it something to run from; its presence in your life could be a catalyst in transforming you into a strong, loving, and wise person.

In Ann Adams' charming book, *The Silver Boat*, we meet a little girl who must travel through a forest filled with monsters to reach a land of light and healing. A guide for her journey tells her that every time she becomes paralyzed by her fears she should stop in her tracks, close her eyes, and say these words, "I must think of what I want rather than what I fear."[4]

There is so much resilience in the human spirit. When you are able to make that journey through those undesired parts of your life, you will most likely discover that your inner strength has been leading you in ways you never dreamed. So you see, you don't always have to journey alone through the forest of fear to find your inner strength. Sometimes it comes to meet you on the way. It becomes a guide accompanying you on whatever path you yet must walk. Focus on your heart's longings more than on your heart's fears. In those deep desires of your heart you will find your strength waiting.

This inner strength can help you discover the gold in your memories. The gold is so surprising. It may be a sudden realization that in spite of wrongs done to you, the key to forgiveness has always been in your possession. Or perhaps it is the welcome recognition that you have learned to set boundaries in your life, and so you are better equipped to ward off harm that might come to you in the future. It can be anything from the remembrance of a moment of beauty to the acceptance of a new vision. My intention in this work is to enable you to discover ways of mining the gold that is hidden in your life.

A Prayer to the God Who Lives Within

Spirit of the Living God,
Move through my life with winds of blessing.
Breathe in me! Wash over me! Empower me!
Fan the embers of hope hidden in my strife.
Blow away all that hinders me
from living an abundant life.

Bright Dawn of God,
Move through my life with winds of blessing.
Reveal! Illuminate! Make known!
Unveil the treasures that are hidden from my sight.
Gift me with stars in the clouds of my night.
Usher me into meadows of delight.

Heart of my heart,
Move through my life with winds of blessing.

Balance! Harmonize! Unify!
Calm the warring factions in my life.
Integrate in me all that has been torn apart.
Merge the joys and sorrows of my heart.

O God of Loveliness,
Move through my life with winds of blessing.
Attend! Transform! Guide!
Massage the places where I am stuck in pain.
Accompany me into the healing spaces.
Refresh me, give me a new name.

Abiding Presence,
Move through my life with winds of blessing.
Soften! Support! Sustain!
Tend the part of me that struggles
with forgiveness, guilt, and doubt.
Gentle whatever in me closes others out.

O Beauty, ever ancient, ever new,
Move through my life with winds of blessing.
Animate! Revitalize! Renew!
Lead me to the gold in my memories.
Rekindle in me that which appears to be lost.
Revive my spirit no matter what the cost.

O Memory of God,
Move through my life with winds of blessing.
Remember! Evoke! Behold!
Recall the lost gifts of my turbulent days.
Lead me to my own tabernacle of memory.
Together let us remember the gold.

EXERCISES

1. Begin with the prayer above.

> Look into your heart's archives. Let memories roll by like
> pictures on a movie screen. When a memory appears that
> takes hold of you, *stop*! Put a frame around that memory.
> Stand back and gaze at it. Take a walk. Have a coffee
> break. Find a chapel or some sacred spot, and sit in re-
> flection. Choose whatever works for you. All this is
> preparation. It is also prayer. When you feel you have
> spent sufficient time musing over this memory, settle
> down in one of your favorite holy places with your note-
> book and begin writing your haiku.

2. After writing your first haiku, let the memories roll again.
   Perhaps you will want to write a second and a third. As
   you create your haiku, try to capture different emotions:
   joy, sadness, delight, disappointment, satisfaction, awareness, etc.

3. If it is helpful for you, find a soul-friend with whom you can
   share these creations.

4. Reading someone else's memoir can help you get in touch
   with your own life-story. Check the bibliography at the
   end of this work. Choose a book to read.

A Mosaic of Memories

Perhaps, I am telling this story in an attempt to heal myself,
to confront what I do not know,
to create a path for myself
with the idea that "memory is the only way home."

—Terry Tempest Williams
Refuge

Walking into the temple of your memory is a way of coming home. You reopen a page of life and listen to the story written on that page. Embracing those memories can be a season of revelation as you recall laughter and tears, jokes and fears, weddings and funerals, births of babies and births of pets. Childhood scars. Grown-up scars. Each has a story of its own. Our personal history contains precious memories that are stored in our souls and our bodies. As we become able to accept and integrate these memories into our conscious life, spontaneous healing occurs. So draw open the curtain. Walk out on the stage. Claim all of life as your teacher.

If you visit the Holy Land you will discover that shrines and churches are often built upon the ruins of ancient hallowed places. So, too, the holy land of your individual life is built upon old ruins, former treasures, forgotten stories, wise ancestors. As you open the book of your life you will discover layers and layers of stories. A story is a vessel of memory, a container of mystery. To understand the mystery, quietly enter the story and listen. You must listen with a depth that takes practice. As you listen, memories will arise. Some of these memories need to be acknowledged so that healing can take place. They are memories of painful events that once needed to be stored away so that you could get on with life. There is much you have forgotten. But now another day has come and you may find in your heart a longing to remember some of those forgotten layers of your life.

Actually there is a wisdom in forgetting. There is a wisdom in distancing ourselves from the sadnesses of the past. For, at times, we are simply not strong enough to deal with the memories, and so they wait for us to grow stronger. Some *secret knowing* deep within honors our trepidation. When we are ready to remember, reminders will come in little ways. Often we are ready to remember long before we are able to be obedient to that readiness. Perhaps that is why the psalmist prays, "In the secret of my heart, teach me wisdom" (Psalm 51:8). And in another psalm, "You increased the strength of my soul" (Psalm 138:3).

In these secret places of my life
let me grow stronger.
Prepare me to see all of my life
and not turn away.

As you move through the pages of your life, some memories will come as a pleasant surprise. A moment long forgotten may return and become an unexpected source of renewal for you. This happened to me recently while spending a few days in the country. One evening, at dusk, the whippoorwill started calling. Immediately I was taken back in time to the memory of my mother and me sleeping out under the stars on summer evenings and listening to the whippoorwill. The whippoorwill was a symbol that brought back a very pleasant memory.

Two other symbols that trigger happy memories for me are freshly cut grass and the aroma that greets me when I pass a bakery. The smell of new mown grass always reminds me of haying season. It was lots of work, but my brothers did the hard work and I got to help in small ways, like riding home atop the hay wagon and rearranging the hay as it was thrown into the loft. The bakery smell transports me back to the womb of the old farmhouse kitchen, waiting for fresh loaves of bread to come out of the oven and knowing that Mama always allowed a first piece while it was still piping hot.

Writing down my memories has often assisted me in discovering the gold in my life. In this chapter I am sharing with you a mosaic of my memories. I like the symbol of a mosaic because it suggests a work of art and, indeed, every person's life is a work of art. As we learn to be present to our experiences each piece of the life that is ours eventually finds a home in our hearts. Sometimes there are pieces we would rather leave out. We think they will surely ruin our mosaic. The colors are too dark and unsettling. Yet to deny any of those pieces is, in some way, to deny who we are; it is a denial of our personal history. It is closing our hearts to revelation.

In sharing with you pieces of my life, remembrances that have come to me through the process of deep listening, it is my hope that you will be motivated to listen to your life. As you learn to replace denial with acceptance you will begin to see the whole of your life as a beautiful painting of many colors. And you will come to understand that, in the end, the shadows and dark places of your mosaic in some mysterious way have added beauty to the work of art that you are.

Memories of various seasons of life come and go. I write what I see as I learn to listen. What I am learning as I write is that these memories are becoming my teachers and guides. What I want to say through these reminiscences is that what has happened in your past is not unimportant. It is not to be thrown away or cast off as futile or unworthy of space in your present life.

Since I'm using the stream-of-consciousness style in my writing, some of what I write may seem to be unconnected. I am not writing my life in chronological order. I'm writing in snippets and I've given each memory a name.

Introducing these memories is one of my favorite folk songs. It was written by J. B. F. Wright. He names his memories "unseen angels." He recalls a mother and father who created for him a home, the memory of which still brings comfort to him in his adult years.

You may remember hearing some of the old folks strumming this song on the guitar or banjo when you were young. Perhaps it was sung in church. Or maybe you sat around a campfire singing "Precious Memories." Tennessee Ernie Ford helped repopularize this song. It remains a haunting melody in my soul.

Precious Memories

Precious memories, unseen angels,
sent from somewhere to my soul;
how they linger, ever near me,
and the sacred past unfold.

Precious memories, how they linger,
how they ever flood my soul,
in the stillness of the midnight,
precious, sacred scenes unfold.

Precious father, loving mother,
fly across the lonely years;
and old home scenes of my childhood,
in fond memory appears.

Precious memories, how they linger,
how they ever flood my soul,
in the stillness of the midnight,
precious, sacred scenes unfold.

As I mine the gold in my memories, I trust you will be enabled to tap into your life's rich resources and create your own mosaic of memories.

LESSONS ON RECEIVING

As a child, one of my heart's desires was to find an arrowhead. My brothers were forever unearthing them when they were out playing in the creek or working in the fields. My father, in particular, while walking behind our old-fashioned, horse-drawn plow seemed to have a knack for mining arrowheads. While plowing the fields one day he found a real beauty, and knowing that I wanted one he offered it to me. But no, I shook my head; I wanted to find my own. He put it in the old hollowed-out rock in our showcase where he always dropped the arrowheads he found.

I never found my own arrowhead. When my father died I went to that hollow rock. Holding it like a sacred vessel I reached in, lovingly fingering the many arrowheads it held. "Papa," I whispered, "please let the arrowhead I take from here be the one you tried to give me." Of course I'll never know for sure, but somehow it doesn't matter now. The arrowhead I chose that day lies on my personal altar. For me, it's a gift from my dad.

There are other memories of searching for treasures that I wanted to find on my own. Seashells, for example. The ones I found were always inadequate. I was looking for one of those classic beauties you see in the tourist shop. A number of times someone tried to give me one and I always refused. I wanted to find it myself.

There were also those Japanese fishing balls that I coveted, large glass balls used as floats. They would break off from fishing boats and eventually make their way to the shore. You see artificial ones in tourist shops and sometimes real ones hanging in nets in seafood restaurants. Once while attending college in Oregon someone tried to give me one. Slow learner that I am, I refused the gift. I wanted to find my own.

A few years ago while leading a retreat at our Center in Arkansas, a woman from New Jersey attended. One day during the retreat she approached me. "I brought you a gift from the sea," she said. In her hands she held an exquisite whelk shell, beautiful, perfectly shaped, spectacularly colored. It was beige, with bits of rusty orange, purples and blues. It was lovely. I looked at that shell and it became a moment of revelation. I remembered how many times in my younger years I had walked the beach looking for such a treasure. Something inside me melted and smiled all in the same moment. It brought back memories. "Thank you," I said. I knew it was a gift I would treasure. It was more than a gift. It has become a symbol for my prayer, a revelation. Later as I sat with the shell in my hand it occurred to me that it is after the storms that you find the *big treasures*. The Japanese fishing balls would be swept to the shore after a big storm. The large shells that I coveted were likely to be more accessible after the storms.

My whelk shell has become one of my teachers. It stirs up memories. How often after the storms of life, treasures have been washed up on my soul's shore. I've been able to see something more clearly and with new eyes because the storm awakened me. It drew forth treasures from my depth, treasures I never knew I possessed.

❧   And what about you? Do you recall a storm in your life
that washed up an unexpected treasure on your shore?

❧   Have you ever received a gift that has become a symbol
and a prayer for you?

What the Trees Taught Me

When I was a kid growing up in Altus, Arkansas, a portion of our school recess was spent sitting around in little circles boasting about what our parents owned, whether it was
a special herd of cattle or a new chain saw. The problem is I
could never think of a whole lot to boast about. One day I
looked out into our forest and thought, "Well, I guess we
own all of these trees!" So I went to my mother and asked,
"Mama, do we own all the trees on our farm?" Seeming a bit
perplexed, my mother assumed that we did. My next question concerned the number. How many? How many trees did
we own? My mother assured me that she really didn't have
time to go out and count them. So I started guessing. One
hundred? I asked. Yes, certainly there were that many, she
said. I kept raising the number. Two hundred? Three hundred? Five hundred seemed a good place to stop, enough to
make my boast somewhat impressive. At school the next day
I tried out my bragging. "Well, we own five hundred trees!"
I announced.

Now in my later years that memory is strangely touching
and a little sad. It has taught me something about that part of
me that wants to possess and own, about my tendency to put,
perhaps, too much value on quantity. How much? How many?
Somewhere along the way I have come to understand the difference between *owning* and *belonging to*. My family no longer
owns the land where I grew up as a child. However, I know the
people who own my childhood forest. I have an invitation to
go there whenever I like. And now when I walk through the
woods or sit by the brook I have a true sense of what it means
to belong to the land. I don't own that land; but I still belong to
it. The aboriginal peoples of the earth understood this too.
They knew very little about possessing; they knew much about

belonging to the land and to one another. I'm not suggesting that ownership is wrong, but I am learning that if, in addition to owning something, you truly belong to it you will treat it with a reverence that will ennoble it; and you will share it. My five hundred trees are finally teaching me.

❧ Spend a little time reflecting on "belonging to" as opposed to "possessing."

❧ Do you have a sense of belonging to something larger than yourself . . . to God . . . to the world . . . a community . . . a family . . . to the earth?

TEACHINGS FROM THE CORNFIELD

Privacy is something I cherish greatly; perhaps this is because I didn't have much as a child. Certainly no one in my home had a private room. Thus, one had to be innovative in creating hiding places for treasures, for letters or diaries. If you longed for some space you could call your own it was up to you to create it. My private room was in the cornfield.

I made a little broom with tall grasses and swept an area clean. An old shirt served as a rug. There in that magical spot I would sit and dream for hours. It was my place of solitude where I would go to think and dream. It was my studio where I could write and read. Books that I remember reading in my cornfield room are *Winnie the Pooh, The Secret Garden, The Wind in the Willows,* and the Nancy Drew mysteries. If you've spent even a little time in a cornfield you will understand that it contains great possibilities for development. The long leaves hang down, gracefully protecting you from sun and even rain. The stalks grow tall enough to give the semblance of a roof.

This was the first room I had to decorate as my very own. I didn't have diaries in those days. There was simply no place to hide them that was safe, so I wrote messages on corn leaves and eventually gave them back to the earth. There is really much joy in that memory, no sadness at all. It was very important for me to write, and when I wanted to write something I didn't want others to read, this seemed to be the safest place. Many of my writings in those days were questions that I wanted to ask but didn't know how. Since I didn't need to store them away forever, I often buried them at the base of the cornstalks. There was, perhaps, one small sadness: every autumn I knew that my cornfield room would become fodder for the cattle. But that was something I just accepted as fact. As I write about this now, the really precious memory for me is my own creativity in using whatever was available to help me find my much-needed space.

❧ What are your memories from the past of *special places* that were like havens for you?

❧ Can you remember ways in which you turned difficult or painful situations into good memories. Do you have some healthy ways for creating the space you need today?

❧ Where are your "cornfields"?

THE MULE

As I become more familiar with computer terminology I begin to understand a little more clearly the workings of the human psyche. Learning to save and delete data, to restore and recycle, I see that a similar process goes on in the psyche.

There are files of memories we perhaps thought we had deleted once and for all; and yet somewhere in the hardware of our inner landscape those memories live on. At the most unexpected moments, given the right symbol, a memory may rise to the surface from the recycling bin of the unconscious and once again be integrated into our consciousness. Such was the case with a certain mule.

For as long as I can remember, a great sadness would descend on me every time I saw a mule. I could be driving out in the country, and just seeing a mule standing in a field would trigger something in me to such an extent that, at times, my eyes would fill up with tears. I would rack my brain for a reasonable explanation, but none would come forth. I simply could not get a handle on what was going on. It was a mystery to me.

A few summers ago I was leading a retreat in Idaho. The room where I was staying had a little veranda and it looked out onto a large meadow where cattle and horses were grazing, and yes, there in the midst of them was a mule.

One afternoon I stood by the fence just a few feet away from the mule. Again I was overwhelmed with feelings of distress and the sense that I desperately wanted to comfort someone. I found myself lying on the ground, making myself very small, and sliding under the fence. Leaning up against a fence post I stared at the mule for a long time. Actually I think I prayed to it asking what on earth was in its ancestry that should bring such sadness to me.

Then suddenly I remembered a story my brother once told me about the only time he saw my father cry. It was a day during the Depression. Papa had paid the last ten dollars he had for a mule to work the fields and it died the next day.

That sad memory had gone into the underground of my soul. It was too painful to hold in my conscious memory. Now I had invited it back to my topsoil. I needed to know the mystery of this sadness, and for some reason having a mule to commune with was healing.

Leaning against the fence post on that June day in Idaho I brought forth some other memories of my father. He had a beautiful tenor voice. I can still hear him, especially during the Easter season, singing with all his heart: "Christ the Lord is risen today. . . ." There was a deep faith in the midst of all our poverty that wove its way through his heart and found its way to mine. That faith still weaves its way through the mosaic of my life. It is not my father's faith; it is my own. Yet in some mysterious way it has grown from the seed of his faith.

Another memory of my father that I hold dear is what I always called his shadow art. Using his hands, in the light of the lamp, he would throw shadows on the kitchen wall in the form of animals. There wasn't an animal I would call out that he couldn't shape. It was always a mystery to me how he did this. It was as though the knowledge was in his hands as I would cry out, "Make a bear, Papa. Make a rabbit. Make a mule!"

The sight of a mule no longer fills me with sadness. Sometimes we have to wade through the sorrows to find the joy. We are all fashioned from the sorrows *and* joys of life.

❧ Can you recall a particular memory of pain from your past that you have worked with in such a way that it is now integrated into your present life?

❧ Are there any symbols that have helped restore past memories for you?

MEMORY OF A MOTHER'S LOVE

Sometimes the most tender of memories comes singing out of the chronicles of my heart all unexpectedly. One day while browsing through one of my favorite junk shops I came upon a number of those old-fashioned flatirons. They were the irons of my childhood. I remembered heating the irons on the wood stove and then using them to press clothes. The memory, however, that took hold of me at that moment had nothing to do with ironing clothes. The sight of those old irons sitting on the dusty shelf that day evoked the memory of my mother's love for me.

It was cold in the old farmhouse where I grew up. Winter winds came whistling through the windows. It was with great reluctance that I would leave the kitchen, the only warm place in the house, on those long winter nights when it was time to prepare for the sandman to arrive. I could dream of being warm soon underneath the covers, but getting there was another story. It seemed as though I was on a journey to the North Pole.

My mother made that cold journey much easier through her ingenuity and loving care. She would take one of the flatirons and heat it on the wood stove. Then she would wrap it in old towels and put it at my feet. That loving episode came surging up from my closed records that day in the antique shop. It is a dear memory and it brings with it gratitude. In my later years, at times, I find myself wishing that I could have been the one putting something warm at her feet, but I was only a child receiving a mother's nurturing love. The memory warms my feet and my heart to this day.

❧   Call up a memory of kindness from days long past.

❧   With what loving gesture might you surprise someone in your life this week?

CONTEMPLATING A BUTTERCUP

One recent morning I was taking the scenic route on my way up to the monastery for Lauds when I met a small yellow flower. It was a buttercup growing out of season. Because it was standing alone it called forth in me a stance of contemplative presence. It would never have caught my eye had it been part of a community of buttercups. It drew me like a magnet and I became prayerfully present just beholding it. I remembered a poem from Rilke in which he suggests that our simple beholding of the object of our delight gives it meaning and brings it to a new birth.[1] It is a healing thought that I gave some kind of completion to that small flower simply by noticing it.

And more than that—as I gazed on that solitary flower I began to recall trees I have known and loved simply because they stood alone. One such tree that comes instantly to my mind is on Highway 9 driving south out of Morrilton toward Perryville, Arkansas. Almost anyone who drives that road will know this tree immediately. It looms up in front of you suddenly like a sentinel. It is beautiful in its solitariness. It is an ordinary tree that is extraordinary somehow precisely because it stands alone. In a forest of trees it would be just another tree, but standing there against the grain fields it becomes a companion on your journey.

All of this musing came about because of a tiny yellow buttercup standing alone, growing beautifully out of season. As I began writing this passage I went back outside and stood in silent vigil with the buttercup. I prayed for the courage to stand alone at times, to withdraw from the crowd that I may carry back to the community the new strength and new vision acquired in solitude.

This morning I went back out to see the buttercup, but it was gone. A rabbit was grazing suspiciously nearby, and I wondered if perhaps it had a buttercup for breakfast.

❧ Allow images to rise in your mind's eye of beautiful pieces of creation that you have noticed because they stood alone.

❧ What is your experience of the growth that comes from solitude?

STARS AND FIREFLIES

There is a memory in my life that is both resplendent and nebulous. An image has fixed itself beautifully in my mind. Although I can't recall all of the conversation and details that centered around it at the time, something about it is abiding and delightful. It is the memory of the first time I saw fireflies. I must have been about four years old and I thought the stars were falling. One might think that stars falling would be a fearful experience, but for me, at that age, the stars were reminders of God. I imagine that whenever I asked grownups where God lived, they must have pointed to the skies, because the night sky and especially the stars were my first image of God.

And so on that summer night when the fireflies were out and about in abundance, I thought God was falling out of the heavens. I remember rushing into the house calling, "Mama, Mama, God is coming!" My excitement is all I remember. I know nothing of my mother's answer, and yet the eternal brightness of that moment, the excitement of God's visitation remains vivid to this day. Every time I pray with this memory some divine voice within me seems to whisper, "Your childhood vision was true. God really was coming!" I have used words to paint a picture of my memory. I call this memory, "The Revelation."

The Revelation

Long ago before her mind
became cluttered with doctrine
there lived a barefoot child
taught only by the mysteries under her feet
and at her fingertips.

"Where is God?"
she kept asking the old ones,
and they would speak of the heavens
pointing upward.
God lived up there, they said.

So she learned to look up
and sure enough, there was God
hanging on every tree branch,
singing from the treetops,
floating in the clouds,
shining in the sun.

But ah, on the night of a great revelation,
looking up she saw God in the darkness.
God came laughing into her life in stars,
stars were everywhere
sliding down the corners of the skies
from all directions,
peeping through the tree branches,
and she began to understand
that you see God best in the darkness
in the great silence of the night.

Then one dusky, summer night
another revelation, new, breathtaking wonder,
her first vision of fireflies,
glowing, shining, lighting up the darkness,
darting, dancing, floating, gliding,
falling, falling stars, falling stars.
"God is falling," she thought,
from the heavens to the earth.

Into the farmhouse she flew,
a disciple of Good News: "Mama, Papa,
God is coming, God is coming!
In the backyard, God is falling!"
The elders came running
with a little less enthusiasm
to the backyard
to see God.

Their answer to her prophetic cry
lives only in the river of her soul,
but this she remembers.
They pointed to the heavens.
And behold, the stars were still there.

And yet beside her,
all around her,
at her fingertips,
God still danced with delight,
here, there, everywhere
God moved with the grace and ease
of fireflies.

Small as she was,
young as she was

back in those pages of her history,
she was enchanted at the mystery
that God had chosen to stay in the heavens
and come to the earth
all in the same moment.
God was everywhere!
But that was before her life
became cluttered up with doctrine.

And now the grownup she's become
is trying to remember
the revelation,
standing on tiptoe again
to see the vision
that has always remained
in the depths of her soul.

✲   What are some of your childhood memories of God?

✲   Take one of these memories and fashion it into a poem.
Try this even if you think you aren't a poet.

INHERITANCE

I hear horror stories of people fighting over an inheritance. When we broke up the old home place there wasn't a lot to fight over. At that time I was a young monastic. I thought I was pretty detached and had given up everything. I wasn't all that interested in souvenirs. However, I did gather up a few things that had special meaning to me, symbols of my childhood on the farm. They are within my reach every day. These treasures rest on my private altar and speak wordless prayers to me:

a cutting from the grapevines in the vineyard
a branch of pine cones from my favorite tree
a little soil

a flat stone from the creek bed
the arrowhead from my father's hollow rock
the seed of the faith of my parents, now resting in my
heart in the form of poetic vision
a tremendous appreciation of nature
the memory of summer evening fireflies

This is my inheritance. I have never regretted that I desired nothing of greater value.

❧ Make a list of the most precious items of your inheritance.

A Favorite Aunt

Sometimes when I feel sad, just thinking about Aunt Annie can work wonders in cheering me up. She lived about a mile away from me, on the south side of our forest. There was a well worn path through the woods from our door to her door. I don't ever remember seeing Aunt Annie with teeth, though I'm sure she must have had them once upon a time. But my precious memory of her is without teeth, and so as far as I'm concerned teeth would have totally ruined her appearance. I never saw her without an apron except in church, and the first apron I owned was made by her. She presented it to me one day when I was helping her pick cherries, and that brings me to another of my favorite memories—picking cherries with her. She had a tree that seemed to never run out of cherries in the summer. I climbed the ladder and picked the high branches; she took care of the bottom of the tree. Then she baked cherry pies and I was always sure to get a small one baked all for me. She and I would have a picnic with it before I returned home.

When she thought I was old enough to keep a secret, she shared this with me. Seems Uncle Bill would send her over to the neighborhood winery now and then to pick up a bottle for him. She decided he was getting too familiar with the bottle, as she put it, and figured out a way to make the wine a little less potent. So one day when she went to fetch his wine she picked up two bottles. She hid one of the bottles and when he was out and about she boiled the wine to weaken the alcohol content. From that day on when she went to get the wine for him she would bury the new bottle in the garden until she could boil it. She would give him the old bottle. Once in awhile he would complain saying, "You know, they just don't make this wine with as much kick as it used to have." She would take a sip of the wine and then she would carry on something awful and agree with him. She'd tell him that the next time she went to that winery she was going to give them a piece of her mind.

I thought she was just about the cleverest woman alive. Spending time with her was one of my dearest childhood pastimes. The memory of her sweet wrinkled face and her bright, sparkling eyes is part of the gold of my inheritance.

🎵   What are your golden memories of people who have been significant for you on your life's journey?

A Friend and Mentor

A note from my journal:

October 18, 1974. Father John Bloms died today. I'll never forget the first time I saw him. I was a young sister on my second teaching assignment at St. Joseph Elementary School in Ada, Oklahoma. The day we arrived a building project was underway, a new church was being built.

The overweight man who met and welcomed us was chewing tobacco and wearing overalls, and I thought he was the janitor or one of the carpenters, but he turned out to be Father John, the pastor. He blew away all images of what I thought a priest was supposed to be like, not only because of the way he was dressed but most of all by the way he thought. He was a free thinker, a man who loved the people of God and wanted them to know that many of the answers to their questions lived right inside their hearts. He was the first person in my life who taught me that my questions were not only acceptable, but valuable. He was a holy rebel, often misunderstood by his community and his church. Now that he has died, I realize I have lost one of the most important teachers of my life. I want to make every effort possible to keep alive in my heart his energetic, humorous, loving, and farseeing spirit.

※ Who have your mentors been, those people who have encouraged you to be our best self?

The Mysterious Visitor

A baffling resident set up tent in my heart as a child. I didn't have a name for it until in my adult years as I began to look back and reflect on my childhood. Now I realize its name was *Love*. How true that, as children, we often feel something in our hearts we cannot name. Most of all I remember the things the *Love* in me wanted to do but never did because it was not modeled in my home. I'm thinking of things like saying, "I'm sorry," or giving my tired mother a hug, or taking hold of my father's hand and walking through the fields with him. I guess there was a way I wanted to massage the weariness, and sometimes the sadness, of my household and I just didn't know how. I don't think children learn to say, "I love you" or "I'm sorry" unless they hear grown-ups say these things. The grown-ups in my household had never learned to express love verbally. They didn't know how to share their vulnerability; and yet in the years I grew up I saw their fragility and their sadness and it terrified me.

Thus I chose other ways of showing love. The way I devised was to bring joy into this family by making them laugh. I became the family clown. Later I had difficulty in determining when I was being authentic and when I was just acting.

As I recall these things now, the *gold* in this memory is the realization of how much love was stored in my young heart, and that it was waiting for someone to reveal to me how to use it. Now in my adult years that revelation is unfolding. It may be too late to shower that love on my own parents, but within easy reach there are still weary mothers and fathers, sisters and brothers. It is never to late to love.

❧ Can you think of a similar experience in your own life, of knowing in your heart that something feels right or wrong but not being able to name it?

❧ What are some things you've been able to pull out of your heart's storage that have been helpful to you in your adult life?

A Memory During the Pause Between Two Sentences

One evening while proclaiming the word of God during Vespers, I was deeply moved as I looked out at the faces of my sisters. There was something immensely precious in those faces staring back at me, listening intently (a few, asleep), a few younger faces sprinkled in among the varying ages. I found myself thinking: "These are my sisters, exasperating and delightful." What a strange mixture we are and how often I have thought of leaving them. I have grown into them now. We have weathered together. And still I have not touched their inner beauty. I have not shared all that I would like to share with them.

I see the face of my ninety-five-year-old aunt, Sister Mary John, staring back at me. So full of wisdom that she does not claim, a woman who encouraged recycling long before we used the term. Her life has been one great longing for sacred ecology though she would never use that term. We have disappointed her because our community has not yet given birth to a reflexologist; but she still has hopes for us. She worries about not remembering, but she seems to remember what she needs to know. She has never forgotten her music. It lives in her soul and one can often hear her playing the harmonica or singing softly as you pass by her room in the infirmary.

And then, there beside her, Sister Columba, a former prioress known affectionately as Clumpy. She always had a bit of a heavy foot while driving. A funny memory I have about her is when she drove up to a filling station to get gas with a police car trailing along behind her all unknown to her. She rolled down the car window and said very matter-of-factly to a somewhat surprised policeman, "Fill it up!" The policeman dutifully turned to the station attendant and repeated her command, "Fill it up!" We never did find out if she got a ticket or just gas.

There is Jane Frances, so full of wisdom and insight, a mentor for many in the community. Bede, a wonderful historian who agonizes over the injustice done to women in the church. She is perhaps one of the few persons in my community I feel totally free to disagree with openly knowing that I'll still be accepted and loved for who I am. Sister Anacletus' face shines forth, and the recollection of her luminous smile every time I give her holy communion is a golden memory. And Christine, who tries with all her gentle power to get us to "lighten up" a bit each day. There is something so good that I could say about each of my sisters, yet how easy it is to forget to say it.

One night, many moons after this life giving pause during Vespers, I saw the movie *El Postino* and was so moved that I decided to write a love poem for my community. I called the poem "Metaphors."

Metaphors

You are the voice singing in my soul
even when I'm not with you.

You are the taste of hope
on discouraging days.

You are the meadow that is sweet
even after you turn into hay.

You are the wind
blowing me out of comfortable ruts.

You are the sun
on cold winter days.

You are the wild
in the whippoorwill's call.

You are sturdy trees
weathering many a storm.

You are the lightening
that splits trees apart.

You are the slow work of God
throughout the ages.

You are my sisters
on good days and difficult days.

❧ Surprise someone that you love with a poem or a haiku
written just for them.

An Unexpected Gift
Notes from my journal:

All through the day I have tried to find a place for you
God, You, the Great Mystery!
    You, in whom I live and move and have my being! I
have tried to fit you into my schedule, forgetting that I
am always in your schedule. And now at last when I am
weary, worn out with too much thought and too much
doing, I am trying to give you these frazzled, leftover

moments before I fall asleep. How kind you have been to me in sleep. I have known few sleepless nights. There is a mysterious trust for you that lives on in my heart, a trust that outlives all my unfaithfulness. Perhaps it is because my life has been filled with so many good people, people who remind me of you. You have given me these people as gift. The gift of each of them is your personal call for me to be a gift for others.

And so tomorrow I fly to Sioux City, Iowa (in response to Mary Michelle's telephone call), to meet Dottie Pecaut who is dying slowly of a rare kind of cancer. Mary tells me that Dottie has found much peace and healing in my writings and her family wants to fly me out as a Mother's Day gift for her so that she can meet me before she dies. How humbling all of this is for me: I, who can't always find time to pray myself. I, who am so scattered and fragmented that I don't take very good care of myself. I am flying out to be a gift for someone who is dying? I've never been given as a gift before, unless that is what was happening on the day of my birth. Still, it all seems so ironic. Tears hide in the depths of my soul. I want to weep! Instead, a peaceful sorrow fills my heart. This may be a call from God.

As I reflect on my visit with this family I realize that I was the one who was given a gift. Memories walk beside me as close as their tears and their smiles. These memories will enrich my life forever. It was such a blessing to be invited so trustingly into someone's sorrow. The bond of love in this family was inspiring, and yet their sorrow was tangible. I walked into the lives of these strangers and was so lovingly accepted. A kinship enfolded me. It was as though I belonged, like I was being given a second family.

One morning some of the family members and I were sitting in a little circle talking about what happens when the soul leaves the body. Suddenly it occurred to me that if we really believe we are temples of God and that God lives in us, as the

Gospel of John (14:21) clearly states, then, when the soul is drawn back to God it follows that in some mysterious way that soul is also drawn into us. Thus a new kind of spiritual presence is born.

As I reflected on my visit with Dottie and her family, a poem made its presence felt in my heart, eventually working its way onto paper as I shaped and molded the words that were given me.

A Gift of Life and Death

I want my death to be a gift, a birth.
When in that final breath
I breathe myself back into God
I want to be drawn into you also,
into the world of stars and earth,
plants and birds and animals,
into the roaring sea.
I want to be an intimate part
of all the universe.
And so, as I am breathed back
into the heart of this world,
into the hopes and dreams
and joys of the people,
into the yearnings
and the tears and sorrows of this world,
my death will be a birth, and a gift.

I want my death to be a gift
and the only way my death
can be a gift, is
if my living is a gift
right now, today
in this frantic, confusing, lovely
messy moment in history.

Oh, just to be here visible, and unhidden,
alive with a hope that has no boundaries,
ever aware of the immense goodness,
at my fingertips, within my reach,
receiving and sharing that goodness
midwiving it into being,
tasting the incredible truth, that
every day is a good day for living
and every day is a good day for dying.
I want my life to be a gift
so that my death can be a gift.

❧ What are some of your golden memories of loved ones
who have died?

❧ Reflect on the gift of your life. What does it mean to you
to be a gift?

❧ Are you afraid of death? How can your death be a gift?

Hidden in Plain Sight

Gold is a mineral that, like with other precious treasures
of the earth, needs to be mined. There are times when, with a
careful eye, gold nuggets can be found on the earth's surface,
but ordinarily finding the gold requires some digging.

There are times when the gold in our memories also
needs to be mined. Some of the treasures in our lives are not always accessible to the heart's memory. As we learn to pay attention to life we discover there is a lot of gold hidden in plain
sight. However, sometimes it takes something jarring and life-
threatening to awaken us to this truth. That "something" happened in my life one day with a telephone call from my doctor.
The following passage is taken from my journal:

> Today, the day after Dottie Pecaut's death, I received some
> news about my own health that I'm trying to process. I've
> never worried much about my health—have always

seemed to be fairly active and healthy, but these past few months I've had to sit up and take notice of my body. My doctor called this morning about a half-hour before I was to leave for Notre Dame for some summer classes. My abdominal/pelvic ultrasound confirms that all does not look well inside me. There seems to be a mass surrounding my right ovary. I had fleeting thoughts of canceling my trip, but the shortness of time and the immediacy of the moment sort of stunned me. I have a consultation appointment as soon as I return.

As I hung up the phone my first thought was, "Well, death is not on my schedule." Then I picked up my calendar, trying to figure out where I would work it in if I had to have surgery. I did all of this lightly, kind of automatically, but it must have been weighing heavily on my mind because by the time I reached St. Louis all I could think of was how precious life is. As I got off the plane I observed the rushing crowd with new eyes. Everyone seemed radiant with life. Every smile was like the light of the sun. The tense and anxious looks drew forth my compassion. And it seemed that every scar, every mole and freckle, was a patch of beauty. Every limp appeared to be a limp of loveliness, a dance.

Faces of loved ones appeared before me like a vision. Among them the image of Dottie Pecaut shone forth like an icon. I walked to the gate that would take me to South Bend using her name as a prayer-mantra. Her gentle presence replaced some of my anxiety. I remembered the poem I wrote for her. Yes, I do want my death to be a gift, but not quite yet. It is life I am pondering now. Suddenly I am passionately aware of the loveliness of life.

My time at Notre Dame turned out to be a kind of retreat. The knowledge that something alien was growing inside me, something that could be malignant and life-threatening, served as a catalyst in drawing forth a poignant appreciation of life.

As I walked the trail around St. Mary's Lake on the campus each day, I became aware of looking at everything as though under a magnifying glass. Seeing it all more clearly, more intensely: the turtles sunning themselves on the log; the swan family with their graceful, commanding glide through the waters; the smile exchanged with others on the trail; every flower, every blade of grass, every lost feather had a clear voice and spoke to me with new intensity. One of my journal entries expresses what a spiritual experience this became for me.

> I try not to be anxious. I practice deep breathing a lot and Jim's meditation class has been just what I needed this week. Life continues to be unusually brilliant in the face of the unknown. The full moon this morning at 5:30 glimmering on the lake seemed like a giant host on a glass paten, a eucharistic moment. I thought of the many eucharists of my life. At some of these eucharists I was wide awake. At other moments I was hardly there, someone else's faith quietly sustaining me. On days when I feel like I'm losing my faith it is comforting to lean toward the faithful—but today, ah, today, I feel immensely faithful. I am changing every moment into eucharist. Christ's presence is in everyone I meet—and I am Christ for them. I walk more aware and with greater gratitude for each step. Nothing is so important as that step and the feel of the earth beneath my feet is a bit of heaven.

A benevolent invasion of my body, more commonly known as surgery, took place on my birthday. It was my first major surgery and calling it a benevolent invasion seemed to take the edge off my anxiety. Although the tumor removed from me was not the totally benign kind I was hoping for, it was completely encapsulated and so my diagnosis was very good.

This experience turned out to be a wonderful means of mining the gold in my memories. Anne Lamott's valuable advice in her book *Bird by Bird* now speaks to me with greater clarity. She says, "My deepest belief is that to live as if we're dying can set us free. Dying people teach you to pay attention and to forgive and not to sweat the small stuff."[2] Now the challenge is to live each day as though I am dying. If I die a little every day, the great death won't be so difficult. As the poem that I wrote for Dottie says, "Every day is a good day to live, and every day is a good day to die." I'm glad that some malignant enemy had not spread through my entire body. And yet, of this I am certain, if that had been the case, I would have learned how to die. Now I am faced with learning once again how to live.

❧   Can you remember any incidents that have been a means of instilling in you a new appreciation for life?

❧   If you were in danger of death, what memories would be foremost in your heart? What would be the gold in your memories?

❧   Today, do some of the things that you would want to do if you knew you had only a short time to live.

MOONS I REMEMBER

The beauty of nature can be immensely healing. Most likely there is some aspect of nature that you find particularly enchanting. For me it is the night sky and especially the moon in all her phases. I remember the presence of many moons in my life. I can often recall where I was and what I was doing on a full moon night.

In one of my earliest remembrances of a full moon night I was nestled on the top of a haystack on our farm in Altus, Arkansas. There were no city lights around to crowd out the darkness, and I distinctly remember the beauty of seeing the barn silhouetted in the moonlight.

Once when I was a young Sister thinking seriously about leaving my community, a moon in Sedona, Arizona shone down on me with such intimacy it seemed to be saying, "Don't go!" I didn't, and have never regretted the voice of that night's moon.

Perhaps one of the most exquisite full moons I've experienced was in Camden, Maine. Victor and Jo Betsy Szebehely had generously given me the use of their house on Penobscot Bay for three weeks of quiet writing space. As I began my writing I was poignantly aware that back at their home in Austin, Texas, Victor was dying of a brain tumor. It was a bittersweet time for me. There was the joy of being in the midst of so much beauty; yet, knowing that Jo Betsy was going through such pain at Victor's bedside created a heaviness in my heart. I was doing much of my writing in Victor's study overlooking the bay and the surroundings seemed imbued with his presence.

A few nights after he died I sat in his study watching the moon rise over the bay. Again I had a strong sense of his and Jo Betsy's presence. Gossamer clouds tenderly enfolded the moon, then gave it back to me again. The path of light upon the waters beckoned to me like God calling me to greater intimacy. Delighting in this immense beauty, again I felt a bittersweet intimacy enfolding me and calling poems from me. Just as Victor had stepped out of his body, I stepped out of mine that night. With all my soul I wrote this poem:

Moonrise on Penobscot Bay

Like a light from some eternal shore
she came climbing over the waters
pushing her way through the clouds
offering the beauty of her fullness
to my waiting eye.

She is dressed in gold
and as she moves
through the canopy of stars
she leaves a golden trail
a path of light upon the waters.

A sweet loneliness fills me
and suddenly I can no longer bear
being on the other side of such beauty.
Softly, without a sound
I step out of my body
moving toward the path of light.
Light as a feather
I float along the golden trail.

She senses my longing
and her gentle magnetic force
lifts me from the great waters.
I am absorbed into her radiance.
For the rest of the night
the two of us move across the heavens
casting glory on the earth.

After a mystical night with the Beloved
I awake in the morning
inebriated with the Light.
I move through the day
on wings of love
tasting still
the sweet loneliness
that one might feel
after a night with God.

SNAPSHOT MEMORIES

In this mosaic of memories I have shared with you a glimpse into my life. It has been a gift freely given. My hope is that you will take time to search out the gifts of your own life as you begin to harvest your memories. Your harvest can be food for your soul.

As you prepare to design a mosaic of your memories, I am suggesting a shortcut to help you get started. All of us have what I call *snapshot memories*, photo picture moments that we never actually got around to photographing. Although you may not have these scenes in your photo-album, you do have them in the tabernacle of your memory.

Here are some examples of snapshot memories from my life.

> sleeping out under the stars with my mother on a summer's night
>
> enjoying a sunset atop a haystack in the barnyard
>
> my little sister running through the tall grasses on a windy day
>
> sunlight falling on my mother's face as she sits by the window mending a shirt
>
> standing before a tree, hanging the moon on whichever branch I chose (I often remember that moment when I hear someone say, "She thinks she hung the moon!")
>
> standing barefoot in patches of bright green moss
>
> a midnight walk with a friend through a dark forest to find the moon
>
> being comforted as a teenager by a cardinal singing in the mulberry tree
>
> a moonrise on Penobscot Bay, Maine
>
> reading *Huckleberry Finn* aloud with a friend
>
> lying in the meadow watching the night fill up with stars
>
> futile childhood efforts to step on my shadow
>
> pieces of a favorite poem I once knew by heart
>
> playing hide-and-go-seek with my cousins

SCRIPTURE MEMORIES

"Faith is confident assurance concerning what we hope for, and conviction about things we do not see" (Hebrews 11:1). Chapter eleven of the book of Hebrews offers us a beautiful summary of the memory of the faith of our ancestors. I love the definition of faith given there. A confident assurance about something we hope for! A conviction about that which we cannot see with our eyes! This kind of faith can only be born out of the hallowed mist of memory. Throughout the ages our ancestors trusted an elusive, aboriginal memory that they could not always name. Offspring of these ancient ancestors, we too find ourselves lured to trust even in the midst of our unknowing and unseeing. A memory of some holy mystery stirring in the universe has taken hold of us. It is not a vivid memory. It is evasive. It is delightfully and painfully vague! It is haunting and holy!

What is this hidden in the universe of our hearts that entices us to stretch, to grow, to hope, to love? Many of our ancestors named this memory *God*. Our God is a haunting memory shadowing our lives in mystery. The "Cloud of Unknowing" which can be grasped only by love and faith, never by thought, hovers over us still.[3] Memory of the "cloud by day, fire by night" which led the people of Israel on their journey of trust, supports our faith to this day (Exodus 13:21).

Remembering the faith of our forefathers and mothers has been my strength on many a difficult day. Their faith has been the ground on which I have stood when I knew not which way to turn. It has been the gold mined from the foundation of their lives. And so at the end of this collage of life, my mosaic would not be complete without calling to mind some of the faithful ones who have sustained me and inspired my prayer life.

Use of the Benedictine prayer form called *Lectio Divina* has made the Hebrew and Christian scriptures an immense source of enrichment for me. My *memory* of nourishment received keeps drawing me back to these sacred pages.

It was Abraham and Sarah's *memory* of God's promise to be with them always that accompanied them on their journey away from the familiar into the unknown (Genesis 12).

It was God's *memory* of Hagar's child, Ishmael, that sent an angel of encouragement to comfort Hagar in her time of exile (Genesis 21:17).

It was Joseph's *memory* of a bond stronger than betrayal that compelled him to offer his brothers the food of forgiveness when they came to him during the famine (Genesis 45).

It was Ruth's *memory* of her devotion to Naomi that called forth from her the prayer, "Wherever you go I shall go . . . " (Ruth 1:16).

It was Peter's bittersweet *memory* of Jesus' love for him that drew out of his soul tears of sorrow (Luke 22:62).

It was the leper's *memory* of being healed that brought him back to Jesus in joyful gratitude (Luke 17:15).

It was the Samaritan woman's *memory* of a drink that transformed her life that led her to become a disciple of Jesus (John 4:39).

It was one woman's *memory* of her sorrow that gave her the courage to risk being ridiculed because of her loving ritual of washing Jesus' feet (Luke 7:38).

It was Jesus' *memory* of the people's hunger that caused him to multiply the loaves and fish (John 6:11).

It was a young boy's *memory* of his ability to share his bread and fish that enabled Jesus to feed the multitude (John 6:9).

It was Jesus' *memory* of the worth of every child that prompted him to gather the children to his side to bless and affirm them (Mark 10:13-16)

It was Jesus' *memory* of the spark of the Divine in each of us that incited him to remind us that we are the salt of the earth and the light of the world (Matthew 5:13-14).

It was Jesus' *memory* of the importance of the anointing at Bethany that caused him to say, "wherever the good news is proclaimed throughout the world, what she has done will be told in her *memory*" (Mark 14:9).

It was Jesus' *memory* of the wavering faith of his disciples that lured him to give them fresh heart through his post-Easter appearances (Luke 24:13-49).

It was Peter and John's *memory* of Jesus that summoned them to heal in his name (Acts 3:1-10).

It is our continual *memory* of these and other saving events that calls us to be disciples of Jesus.

When we gather around the altar to break open the Word and share the Bread of Life it is in memory of Jesus that we come together. And so it seems to me that it is always *memory* that finally leads us home. Like the prodigal son we are drawn home because we remember our hunger. Hunger for things that do not satisfy leads us to our deeper hungers. Thus all our longings can be used for our good. God takes our hungers, however imperfect they may be, and remembers our original longing. It is the memory of our hunger that leads us home.

I believe that it is our *memory* of God's sanctifying grace, planted deep in the core of our beings, that leads each of us finally to turn toward the source of that grace. This is evident in the lives of saints and prophets of all ages. This is why we have people like Dorothy Day and Mother Teresa, Catherine of Siena and Francis of Assisi, Oscar Romero and Maximilian Kolbe, Harriet Tubman and Martin Luther King Jr. They remembered that they were to be light for the world and salt for the earth. They remembered the gospel of Jesus. They discovered that their lives were full of grace. They allowed the gold in their memories to transform them and draw them into the heart of the world. They remembered the magic of love. And now, as we remember them, they become our mentors.

> O Beauty ever ancient, ever new! You are the designer of the portrait of our lives. Each of us is an original work of art. We have come from the kiln of your hand—unique, beautiful and good, yet unfinished. Our "unfinished-ness" is your way of asking us to be partners in our own creation. In the living of our lives, some of the pieces of our mosaic have been marred. Some are slightly flawed. This wound in us may have taken place because of our own weakness or it may have happened because of someone else's poor vision.
>
> Remind us, dear Mender of Lives, that even the pieces we want to rip out and throw away, you accept. Not only

do you accept them, you cherish them. You reveal to us ever so gently that they are part of the fabric of our lives. They have a right to be there.

Help us to look at each person as a work of art. Be in our seeing that we might gaze upon ourselves and one another with the eyes of an artist. Teach us to behold rather than merely to look at one another. In our beholding we will begin to understand that the shadows, the rough places, the many colors and experiences are all part of the beauty of the mosaic.

Loving God, just as you have not turned away from us never let us turn away from the beauty of our lives.

EXERCISES

1. Find a quiet place. Close your eyes and glance back through the pages of your life. Gather up some of the unphotographed moments for your enjoyment. In your journal, create your own list of snapshot memories. Try to be unusually attentive to beauty this week.

2. Use the list of memories you created for your prayer tomorrow. You may be tempted to ask, "But how do I pray with these memories?" Ponder that question and decide for yourself.

3. Choose one of your snapshot memories and write a haiku.

4. Now choose one of the haikus that you composed at the end of the first chapter. Write more extensively about it. Try not to compose, but just pick up your pen and let it flow. This can be the beginning of the chapter of your own mosaic of memories.

5. Check in your heart to see if there might be a poet imprisoned there. Free it! It is not what you write that makes you a poet. It is rather *how you see.*

Memories of Books I Have Loved

For some of us, books are as important
as almost anything else on earth.
What a miracle it is that out of these
small, flat, rigid squares of paper
unfolds world after world after world,
worlds that sing to you,
comfort and quiet or excite you.
Books help us understand
who we are and how we are to behave.
They show us what community and friendship mean;
they show us how to live and die.
They are full of all the things you don't get in real life,
wonderful lyrical language, and quality of attention. . . .
An author makes you notice, makes you pay attention,
and this is a great gift.

—Anne Lamott
Bird by Bird

For as long as I can remember, books have been a haven and refuge for me. Reading a book is like walking into a new and sometimes magical land where I feel safe enough to get lost. I meet wonderful people who are trying to make sense out of some of the same things I struggle with. As I visit new places I am introduced to other cultures and religions. I learn new customs.

When I'm reading a book I enjoy, I can enter into it so fully that I live with the characters throughout the reading. I meet them at the breakfast table, in the supermarket, and on the street. They get under my skin and into my heart.

I tend to feel a special connection with people who are reading the same books I'm reading. It is as though we are spending time in the same circle of friends. Once when a friend and I were both reading Tony Hillerman's Navajo mystery stories I surprised her with a gift under the Christmas tree. It was a scarf from the southwest with a little note reading, "Merry Christmas from Jim Chee and Joe Leaphorn." She was delighted to receive a gift from these two colorful detectives in Hillerman's stories. Of course, this gift and its message would have made no sense to someone unfamiliar with Hillerman's characters.

Fiction is a marvelous vehicle of truth. I find myself in the characters. As I walk with them through their deaths and resurrections I receive new insight into the foibles and loveliness of my own life. I miss the characters when the book is finished, and so I often find myself reading the last chapters very slowly. When I finish a story that I've truly treasured, I wait at least a week before beginning a new one. It's a kind of reverence for the "book friends" I've grown to cherish. I want to live with them a little longer. I want to remember them and continue learning from them. I don't want to say good-bye too quickly.

Many of the books I read are nonfiction. I am especially fond of travel stories, biography, geography, ecology, memoirs, spirituality, and poetry. Each book is an entrance into a new world. The author stretches me. My world becomes a little larger. The door of my heart opens wider. Authors are very special people. They often lead me to the gold in my memories.

I have fond memories of a friend and my reading out loud to one another. When we would take turns reading *Huckleberry Finn* or perhaps *Winnie the Pooh,* the book seemed twice as good. I've discovered, however, that not everyone likes to be read to, and that is just fine. So you'd best check out the taste of your friends before you start reading to them. There is simply no sense in wasting a good read on someone who doesn't appreciate it.

This book would seem incomplete without reference to some of the books that live on in my memory. Most of these books I have read more than once. They have sustained and nurtured me many a day. They touch a chord in me, and I can't get their melody out of my soul. They call me to prayer. They stir me to wonder, drawing forth both laughter and tears. As I walk through their pages, the authors, whom I suspect are often writing about their own lives, inspire, challenge, console, and encourage me. The books I'm choosing to share with you are ones that have been a healing force in my life. For some reason they refuse to leave me. They return in my greatest moments of need. They come bringing memories. I remember how I felt when I first read them. Sometimes I can even remember where I was when I finished the book and what kind of day it was. The memory of a book so kind to one's soul is pure gold.

THE SECRET GARDEN

When I was young and it was past my bedtime, I used to sneak a flashlight and a book into bed with me. After my sister was asleep, I would curl up in a little ball, camouflaged under the covers, and read myself to sleep.

It was under the covers (and out in the cornfield) that I first met Mary, Colin, and Dickon in *The Secret Garden*. My enchantment with this book has never weakened. In my adult years it speaks to me in even deeper ways; it wakes up a magic within that has the tendency of getting lost in grown-ups.

Recently a friend and I designed a retreat based on *The Secret Garden*. Such down-home wisdom can be found in this classic, food for meditation on practically every page. Perhaps you can identify with some of the characters in this story. There are Mary and Colin, neglected and self-centered until the wondrous secret garden transforms them both. And there is Dickon, unselfish, loving, natural as the flowers and animals he so loves. You will meet Lord Craven, Colin's father, who in locking the garden has locked himself up in a world of grief and isolation. He remains imprisoned until the magic of the children's love sets him free.

The key to the secret garden was so much more than just the rusty old key Mary found that opened the door. The real key that opened up all the locked hearts in this story was the magic of relationships restored—love and life discovered. I, too, have memories of special keys in my life that have opened the locked doors of my heart, and again, I am blessed by these memories.

There are times when we are inclined to think that the garden of our lives is dead, just as Mary first thought the garden she entered was dead. It was only after investigation that she detected all of the hidden life.

> She thought she saw something sticking out of the black earth—some sharp little pale green points. . . . She knelt down to look at them.
>
> "Yes, they are tiny growing things and they might be crocuses or snowdrops or daffodils," she whispered. "Perhaps there are some other ones coming up in other places," she said. "I will go all over the garden and look."
>
> . . . She went slowly and kept her eyes on the ground. She looked in the old border beds and among the grass, and after she had gone round, trying to miss nothing, she had found ever so many more sharp, pale green points, and had become quite excited again.
>
> "It isn't a quite dead garden," she cried out softly to herself.

She didn't know anything about gardening, but the grass seemed so thick in some places where the green points were pushing their way through that she thought they did not seem to have room enough to grow. She searched about until she found a rather sharp piece of wood and knelt down and dug and weeded out the weeds and grass until she made nice little clear places around them.

"Now they look as if they could breathe," she said, after she had finished with the first ones. "I am going to do ever so many more." [1]

⅄   Using the image of a garden as a symbol for your life, walk through your own garden searching for those little pale green shoots. Is there anything in your garden of life that needs room to breathe?

⅄   What (or who) are the keys that have unlocked some of the hidden potential in your life?

THE WIND IN THE WILLOWS

Anyone who can write with such soul about four animal creatures who are ordinarily detested by humans must have a poet's heart and a wonderful imagination. Long ago when I was first introduced to Mole, Rat, Toad, and Badger in *The Wind in the Willows*, I fell in love with them immediately, but I had a special affection for Mole. Perhaps my compassion for them was born on the day when, as a child, I discovered that they were unable to see and had to live underground. I have since learned that those of us who live above ground don't always see very well either. Perhaps Kenneth Grahame, the author, who was shuffled from relative to relative in his early years, realized that too. In the solitude of his childhood, perhaps he had time to befriend the creatures who didn't live in "people" houses. He describes these animals' houses in great detail. And indeed, they are comfortable little homes. I wonder what Grahame is saying in all of these descriptions. Is he describing something of what he missed in a cozy dwelling, a place to be comfortable, a place to feel at home?

At any rate, he hooked me immediately when he described Mole as wearing a black velvet suit. And how could one not love a rat who writes poetry? As I read about the meanderings of Mole and Rat I am reminded of some of my own childhood meanderings.

Kenneth Grahame's words are like music. He was one of my childhood inspirations. Listen to the poetry in this description of Mole's first meeting with Rat.

> The mole had been working all morning spring-cleaning his little home. . . . Spring was moving in the air above and in the earth below and around him, penetrating even his dark and lowly little house with its spirit of divine discontent and longing. It was small wonder, then, that he suddenly flung down his brush on the floor, said . . . "Hang spring-cleaning!" and bolted out of the house without even waiting to put on his coat. Something up above was calling him imperiously, and he made for the steep little tunnel. . . . So he scraped and scratched and scrabbled and scrooged . . . working busily with his little paws and muttering to himself, "Up we go! Up we go!" till at last, pop! His snout came out into the sunlight, and he found himself rolling in the warm grass of a great meadow. . . .
>
> He thought his happiness was complete when, as he meandered aimlessly along, suddenly he stood by the edge of a full-fed river. Never in his life had he seen a river before. . . . The mole was bewitched, entranced, fascinated. By the side of the river he trotted as one trots, when very small, by the side of a man who holds one spell-bound by exciting stories; and when tired at last, he sat on the bank while the river still chattered on to him, a babbling procession of the best stories in the

world, sent from the heart of the earth to be told at last to the insatiable sea.

As he sat on the grass and looked across the river, a dark hole in the bank opposite, just above the water's edge, caught his eye, and dreamily he fell to considering what a nice snug dwelling-place it would make for an animal with few wants and fond of bayou riverside residence. . . . As he gazed, something bright and small seemed to twinkle down in the heart of it, vanished, then twinkled once more like a tiny star . . . then, as he looked again it winked at him, and so declared itself to be an eye; and a small face began gradually to grow up round it, like a frame round a picture. A brown little face with whiskers. A grave little face, with the same twinkle in its eye that had first attracted his notice. Small neat ears and thick silky hair. It was Water Rat!

Then the two animals stood and regarded each other cautiously.

"Hullo, Mole!" said Water Rat.

"Hullo, Rat!" said Mole! [2]

And so began the acquaintance of Rat and Mole. Imagination is a precious gift. Kenneth Grahame had a bountiful supply. He has blessed many children and adults with his precocious animal characters. I am immensely grateful for the gift of imagination. It has enriched my life in so many ways.

One of the reasons why *The Wind in the Willows* has always been so special to me is because the first dream I truly remember occurred while I was reading it. A humorous memory from my childhood is the telling of our dreams at the breakfast table. I didn't remember dreams at that time in my life, and so not to be outdone by my sisters and brothers, I made up my dreams. They were wonderful and quite flamboyant, and on occasion I would be accused of making them up. I decided that I could legitimately say they were real because they were my daydreams instead of night dreams. My family didn't have to know what kind of dream I was telling.

In my dream I was walking to school. I must have been quite fascinated with Mole's velvet suit. I put my hand in my pocket and felt something velvet. I knew immediately that it was Mole. I was concerned that if Sister discovered I had a mole in my pocket she would take it away, so I decided to just keep it a secret and no one would know it was there. However, after awhile I couldn't endure keeping the secret any longer and probably wanted to show off a little. So I took Mole out of my pocket and put him on my desk. Naturally there was a commotion when the other children saw it and then, of course, my teacher saw it. My worst fears were realized when she said I had to put it outside. I said, "But he's wearing his best velvet suit!" That didn't impress her. I was standing at the school-room door with the mole clutched to my heart when I woke up, and I was whispering, "Velvet. . . ." That dream would never have lingered in my mind into my adult years except for *The Wind in the Willows.*

❦   Reflect on the value of imagination. How can imagination enrich your prayer life?

❦   What is your favorite book from your childhood days?

❦   Can you recall a dream about animals?

❦   Reread the description of Mole meeting Rat. Write a descriptive memory about your first meeting with someone.

THE FAITHFUL GARDENER

I never really know whether I'd like to own a book until I've read it. One cloudy afternoon when the muses seemed to have gone on vacation, my restlessness drove me to the public library. I walked in and out of rows and rows of books hoping one of them would choose me. *The Faithful Gardener* caught my eye. It wasn't shelved properly. I rescued it from its orphaned state, took it to one of the reading stalls, and got lost in its pages. I finished it in one sitting, checked it out, and read it again the next day.

It's author, Clarissa Pinkola Estes, comes from a long line of storytellers. In the beginning of the book she quotes an old family blessing which suggests that anyone still awake at the end of a night of stories will become the wisest person in the world.

The Faithful Gardener is a story within a story within a story within a story. . . . All are stories of loss and survival. The story is about her beloved uncle who survived the horrors of the Nazi labor camps. He came home with memories too awful to speak of, but as Clarissa explains in her little book, "people have to speak of what has hurt them; otherwise the war beast jumps out in nightmares. . . . "[3] Her Uncle Zovar brought the seeds of many stories with him across the great ocean, and so he spoke in stories. Some of the stories told of the earth's hospitality and how, after a great fire, seeds wait in the fallow earth for the right moment to grow again into a forest. In the telling of the stories, in the waiting with the fallow land, he came to live again.

This is a book about that within us which can never die; it is a story about the gold of our lives which endures forever. Like a healing balm it is fine tonic for a weary soul. In moments of doubt and desolation the wisdom of this story returns to me, offering hope. Uncle Zovar's life gives witness to a steadfast power within us that lies fallow in certain seasons only to rise again.

> I am certain that as we stand in the care of this faithful force, that what seemed dead is dead no longer, what has seemed lost, is no longer lost, that which some have claimed impossible, is made clearly possible, and what ground is fallow is only resting, resting and waiting for the blessed seed to arrive on the wind with all Godspeed.
>   And it will.[4]

After reading this book five times, I decided it was time to purchase it. I gave it a home on my bookshelf. Most likely there will come a day when it will travel to someone else's bookshelf, but for now it is a welcoming presence that feeds my memories.

※ Is there a special story that stirs up memories in you?

※ How would you describe that within you which cannot die?

※ Have you ever planted a tree? Make plans for the planting.

LETTERS OF THE SCATTERED BROTHERHOOD

A visit to a used bookstore acquainted me with this dear classic. Edited by Mary Strong, it is a collection of anonymous letters, pieces of spiritual advice, and encouragement—timely for all ages and all religions. I found it when I was going through a time of spiritual aridity. Nothing seemed to be working for me. Heart and soul utterly barricaded, no Beloved in view!

It has been my practice during seasons of barrenness to search for something old rather than something new. Somehow I know, in the part of me that contains reservoirs of hidden wisdom, that what I am longing for is not to be found in the latest fad. Rather, it is to be rediscovered in something ancient yet ever new, something that needs to be rekindled and hallowed again. I have always found this to be so.

Finding this book was like finding water in the desert. Almost every page contained truths I knew but had forgotten. I have always believed in small miracles such as being able to find something needed at just the right time. The day my eyes fell upon *Letters of the Scattered Brotherhood* one of those small miracles was taking place. As I picked it up and started browsing through it, it became clear in my mind that God was visiting me.

Here is a taste of the wisdom in this spiritual classic.

Today we speak of the realization of the black and white of daily living; now one thing and now another. . . . They are very real while they last, these times of fermentation and doubt. It seems to you that there can be no light or hope and the days are gray and dark. *Much of this is steam rising from you and you make your own fog.* When understood it is a sign of growth; but you will feel better, feel cleansed when you have the understanding to ponder on the strangeness of these states, as being unreal and not of truth. . . . Your release lies in taking these moments, both the star moments and the nettles and in holding them in each hand while you consider them. . . .

You are here, now, at this place, at this time, in this room, in your world . . . and you have never been at this moment before. Well, then, take this moment and instead of letting it wing through the mind as nothing, receive it as a divine gift and place it in the chalice, holding it up as high as you can reach. . . . This is how inspiration will pour into your life for, oh, it is so important not to drop the moments on the floor. Hold them up into the light when all the currents and tides are against you; every time you raise a low impulse to the highest, those nearest you are lifted and changed.[5]

❧ Can you identify with the statement that at times we make our own fog?

❧ Reflect on some of your star moments as well as your nettle moments. What have you learned from these moments?

❧ The best way to save a moment is to be present to that moment. Let that be part of your practice today.

❧ Is there a book that lingers in your memory as being one that you found at just the right time? If so, might it be rewarding to re-acquaint yourself with its wisdom?

THE LOST WORLD OF THE KALAHARI and THE HEART OF THE HUNTER

Perhaps no author has touched me as deeply as Laurens van der Post. Upon discovering him I thought, "Where have I been that it has taken me so long to meet this wonderful author?" When he died December 15, 1996, my one regret was that I never wrote him the letter that was in my heart telling him how much his works enriched me and kept my dreams alive. He is the first author I ever thought about writing.

He grew up in South Africa and was nurtured with stories of the ancient times and its peoples by his Bushman nurse, Klara. These stories touched something deep in his spirit and remained in his memory like a sweet fragrance, always staying close enough to rekindle the flame within.

In *The Lost World of the Kalahari* he shares a certain anguish that he felt over the plight of the Bushman and his inability to get the grownups of his day to talk about it. He found himself wondering if his ancestors had anything to do with the extermination of the Bushman. When he questioned them, their silence confirmed his greatest fears. We are often silent about that which we cannot bear to speak. The answer that he sometimes received was enough to break one's heart . . . "but you see he just would not be tamed." To tame another person is to bend them to our will, to try to make them as we are. Alas, I fear that is death.

And so the young van der Post was haunted by a terrible truth and a terrible beauty. He made a promise when he was fourteen years old: when he was grown up he would go into the heart of the great Kalahari and search out the vanishing Bushman. It was a dream that followed him through his years as a soldier and as a prisoner of war. These books are about the promise that he kept.

In his writings about the aboriginal peoples of South Africa, the Bushman, he touches the heart of what has gone wrong in our world. In lovely, lyrical language van der Post explains that the predicament our world faces today is the loss of *first spirit*, or loss of soul.

The primitive world regarded the preservation of first spirit as the greatest, most urgent of all its tasks. It designed elaborate rituals, ceaselessly fashioned myths, legends, stories and music, to contain the meaning and feed the fire of the creative spirit.[6]

Is that not what all cultures and religions try to do in a certain sense, preserve something precious of the old ways even while opening to the process of the unfolding life which will bring forth new seeds from the old?

Make no mistake: As I read these wonderful epics, I have no desire to go live in the bush. Yet I am touched to the core by these stories. I believe the reason I am so moved is a deeply spiritual one. Each of us, in our own way, is called to keep alive that *first spirit*. That within us which is most ancient, the aboriginal spirit born on the first day of creation, is crying to be remembered in our lives. "There is a dream dreaming us," is an old Bushman saying. That dream is as old as God. A golden memory of what is most important since the dawn of time abides in the universe. May we remember.

I offer you the following quote from *The Heart of the Hunter*:

Intellectually, modern man knows almost all there is to know about the pattern of creation in himself, the forms it takes, the surface designs it describes. He has measured the pitch of its rhythms and carefully recorded all the mechanics. From the outside he sees the desirable first object of life more clearly perhaps than man has ever seen it before. But less and less does he experience the process within. Less and less is he capable of committing himself body and soul to the creative experiment that is continually seeking to fire him and to charge his little life with great objective meaning. Cut off by accumulated knowledge from the heart of his own living experience, he moves among a comfortable rubble of material possession, alone and unbelonging, sick, poor, starved of meaning. How different the naked little Bushman, who could carry all he possessed in one hand! Whatever his life lacked, I never felt it lacked meaning. Meaning for him died only when we bent him to our bright twentieth-century will. Otherwise, he was rich where we were poor; he walked clear-cut through my mind, clothed in his own vivid experience of the dream of life within him.[7]

❧ Have you ever experienced your possessions keeping you from being your original and truest self?

❧ What do you think van der Post means when he says we are suffering from a loss of soul?

❧ Is there a dream in your life that still needs your attention?

No Enemies Within

Like many people on the journey, I've had to work with "stuff" in my life. Stuff that sometimes has the word "disorder" at the end of a series of other words, issues of fear, guilt, procrastination, frozen feelings, addiction. It's easy, at times, to feel that one's house has been invaded by enemies. Then unexpectedly, a book comes along that is almost as good as your therapist—or maybe better. There are so many self-help books published today that I tend to be wary of them. Yet I do believe that "God helps those who help themselves."

There is so much courage in us, and we need to make its acquaintance. Dawna Markova introduced me to my courage and wisdom in her book *No Enemies Within*. With humor and intensity she teaches us how to be in relationship with the wounds of the past in such a way that they become our teachers. As I was browsing through the book I came across a paragraph that convinced me the study of this book would be worth my while.

As you may already have guessed, I am a passionate advocate of the possibility for change. I believe your turning point, dear reader, is a moment that invites you to remember, reclaim, speak, create, heal, share, and teach your own truth. I would like to accompany you on your search for the ally that hides within the enemy. I would like to help you replace that cage with a nest of your own design, to home the feathered mysteries that live waiting inside your darkest corners, yearning for release.[8]

As I beheld those words a voice that was my own said, "Yes! I want those *feathered mysteries* within me to have a home. I don't want to remain trapped in the pain." Even as I write these words, I realize that what I'm referring to indirectly is the gold in my memories. It waits inside me to be known—when the time for knowing is right.

❧ Is there a cage in your life that needs to be replaced with a nest?

❧ What feathered mysteries in your dark corners are yearning for release?

❧ Reflect on this age-old saying: "God helps those who help themselves." How do you interpret this?

Start Where You Are

This book was a great find. It has been very helpful for me in living community life where you live in close proximity with many persons. I finally investigated it because one of my friends found it so valuable. I sometimes think one of the nicest things we can do for one another as friends is to lead each other to good books.

Start Where You Are is a book about awakening the heart to compassion. The author, Pema Chodron, is a Buddhist nun. She uses a meditation practice designed to help us connect with the openness of our hearts. The meditation practice is called *tonglen*, which means "taking in and sending out." Thus instead of always trying to protect ourselves, our "soft spot," with *tonglen* we could let ourselves feel what it is to be human.

She also presents very practical teachings on compassion centered around fifty-nine traditional Tibetan Buddhist slogans, such as:

Always meditate on whatever provokes resentment.

Be grateful to everyone.

Change your attitude, but remain natural.

Don't talk about injured limbs.

Examine the nature of unborn awareness.

These *lojong* teachings assist us in awakening the heart. *Lojong* means "mind-training." The following passage explains more explicitly how this works:

> The next two slogans, "Always maintain only a joyful mind," and "If you can practice even when distracted, you are well trained," go hand in hand. The first is saying that if you regard everything that arises as fuel to wake up, you can remain cheerful. The second is saying that you are well trained if you can do that, use everything in your life to wake yourself up rather than put yourself to sleep, no matter what.
>
> If you feel completely caught up and are spinning off into a misery scenario, the slogan, "If you can practice even when distracted, you are well trained," can remind you to start to work with *tonglen*, to breathe in the mishap or the misery as a way of developing compassion for yourself and as a way of beginning to understand other people's pain as well. You can use the distraction to bring yourself back to the present moment, just as a horse rights itself after losing balance or skiers catch themselves just as they are about to fall. Being well trained means that you catch yourself and come back to the present.[9]

A practical example of how I have used *tonglen* meditation is in the area of keeping a regular schedule for my writing. When I slip into my undisciplined state, instead of heaping shame onto the guilt I already feel, I now breathe in the reality of my difficulty in staying on schedule. Then I breathe out compassion and acceptance not only for myself but for all who struggle with this same issue.

This can be most helpful in the area of forgiveness. You catch yourself with hateful thoughts toward someone. Breathe in those thoughts and the reality that you are capable of having them, then breathe out compassion for yourself and for all who struggle with forgiveness.

This meditation is not just for yourself; it is for the whole world. I'll never be able to explain how beneficial this has been for me, so I encourage you to find the book and practice. I particularly like the fact that Pema Chodron, throughout this work, encourages us to lighten up, to laugh at ourselves lovingly.

As a Christian I find it very important to always keep my heart open and grateful for the teachings of all the world religions. I always try to keep something from the eastern traditions right beside my Bible.

❧ How do you awaken your heart to compassion?

❧ How do you need to lighten up?

❧ What book has a friend helped you discover?

PASSION BELOW ZERO

I hardly know what to say about this wonderful collection of essays. I suppose it would be best to tell you a little about the author whom I know only through his writings. A few years ago a friend began to subscribe to a weekly newspaper for me, *The Bugle* of Island Park, Idaho. He told me I probably wouldn't be interested in the fishing news but to check out the editorials. I did! They stole my heart. This collection of essays entitled *Passion Below Zero* is some of the editorials from *The Bugle*.

The author—a bit of a recluse—is David Hays. In his weekly columns he uses the pen name *Seldom Seen*. He is a hermit both by circumstance and choice. I think he's probably a Ph.D. hippie gone beautifully wild. I love his humor, his vulnerability, his wisdom and honesty. He writes in prose, but much of it sounds like poetry. It doesn't take long to understand that he has a poet's soul. I think he is a poet because of the way he sees.

If you read *Passion Below Zero* with an open heart, it just might turn into spiritual reading or meditation material for you. There is substance here. It is deeply personal; yet you can easily find yourself in the spaces between the words. I even sneak a few of his columns into our dining room for monastic table reading on occasion. Before I continue let me introduce David Hays to you:

> I live at the end of a road. I chose it to be so because I am neither social enough to require companionship nor rude enough to deny it, and if you live at the end of a road folks rarely drop by without serious reason. . . .
>
> I was born by the sea but was never of it; it moved too much to kindle my imagination and its protean moods depressed me. The mountains were so far off in my childhood that they were merely a ripple on the eastern horizon, but I spent many summer days watching the clouds build there and dreamed of going.
>
> I went. It has been a very long and twisted road to this place and I have been often lost and afraid. I have been to foreign lands and learned their languages and ways, been to northern Montana at sixteen to harvest wheat on the endless prairie, worked the tow boats in New Orleans, lectured at Columbia University, sang the blues in Memphis. I have cared deeply and often, given my heart away a hundred times never to have it taken . . . until now.

I live at the end of a road in a place called Last Chance, and since last week the irony has become amusing and I am troubled no more by where to go seeking. I can see the Tetons from my front door and feel the roots of this land lain gently across my days. It is a season to be thankful and I dearly, dearly am.

The pilgrim has come home.[10]

David writes with passion, of love lost and love found. He lives in a place where the summers are short and the winters are long. The growing season there, he says, is about twelve minutes long. It is obvious that his growing season is much longer. If there is anything that rings clear in his writings it is that his life has been an adventure, a process of losing and finding. He seems to have come through fire and water—not unscathed, yet not bitter. A quote from Tolkien could perhaps be true of David, "His grief he will not forget, but it will not darken his heart, it will teach him wisdom."[11] Yes, wisdom has definitely become his companion.

Here is a person who has learned to be happy and poor. He lives in a one-room cabin with the richness of the mountains surrounding him. He lives the simplicity that many of us talk about, but seldom practice. His words are part of the gold in my memories.

Learning how to be happy is like learning any other skill: figure out what it is you want to make or do, get together the tools and things you need, and practice a lot. I heard a local wag the other day saying money couldn't buy happiness but it could buy living well, and doing that could make him happy. I'd heard that before, but tools like money seem to be out of the question for someone with my lifestyle and destiny, so a few years ago I proposed to discover what living well (for me) was, and how to get there without paying for it in cash.

At the time I decided this it was forty-five below outside, with a ripe north wind, and the cat and I were huddled inside the thin cabin in front of the pesky stove on a platform of books, since the thinner carpet had been given over to frost. We were out of coffee, almost out of water, the pipe tobacco was as meager as the pantry, the storm had been howling for two days and seemed to be just getting warmed up, the roads were blown shut in three states. . . .

There being little else to do, I pulled the blanket closer and pondered happiness. The books we nested on were good ones, books you like to read again and will. The inexpensive prints icing up on the walls were of good taste and required being looked at often and in different lights. The wind coming in through the cracks in the walls smelled fresh and clean. I decided it was a nice day, a nicer day than I had enjoyed in many other places, and I have been many other places. As I got up to break up the last piece of furniture for stove wood, I decided that I liked it here because I had chosen to be here, and be here in this way. It wasn't handed to me. At this midpoint in my life I had decided to take responsibility, finally, for where and how I am. As the pot on the stove scorched the snow I was trying to melt for dried wildflower-weed tea, I look around and noticed I was living well; no question about it, I knew how to live well.

I got up and looked out the window as best I could and grinned about knowing how. As the snow swallowed the last of the truck, I knew I had arrived at living well and being happy.[12]

Now I don't know if David truly burned up the last piece of furniture on that cold winter day when he claims to have arrived at the state of knowing how to live well and be happy. Perhaps he is speaking in hyperbole and saying a little more than he literally means in order to get us thinking, as storytellers often do.

What I do know is that many of us have lost a lot of life in trying to make a living. These humorous and wise essays help me to laugh at myself. They also serve to stir up the sleeping embers of longing and hope in my soul.

❧ Have you experienced the need to make a living get in the way of making a life?

❧ Name a piece of wisdom that you have learned from the struggles of daily living.

CRY THE BELOVED COUNTRY and TOO LATE THE PHALAROPE

Alan Paton's *Cry the Beloved Country* is insightful, probing, dynamic, a piercingly beautiful novel. It is the deeply moving story of a Zulu pastor, Stephen Kumalo, seeking his elusive prodigal son, Absalom. It is also the story of a precious bonding that takes place as Msimangu, a younger priest, befriends and accompanies the old father in his search. The setting is South Africa just before apartheid became official policy in 1948. It is a critical time for the land and its people. The country is being torn apart by racial injustice. Fear reins. Love waits.

> Have no doubt it is fear in the land. . . . Who can enjoy the lovely land, who can enjoy the seventy years, and the sun that pours down on the earth, when there is fear in the heart? Who can walk quietly in the shadow of the jacarandas, when their beauty is grown to danger? Who can lie peacefully abed, while the darkness holds some secret? What lovers can lie sweetly under the stars, when menace grows with the measure of their seclusion?[13]

The tears that I wept while reading this book were cleansing. I was called to examine my own fears and claim my sorrows. This unforgettable story stirs up love and encourages forgiveness and compassion. Although it has been many years since I've read this book, memories linger. One especially touching scene that I've never forgotten is that of a younger white priest, Fr. Vincent, trying to counsel and console the old black priest. The priest's son has killed a very good white man, although out of fear, rather than intent to kill. Fr. Vincent says to the old priest:

> —My friend, your anxiety turned to fear, and your fear turned to sorrow. But sorrow is better than fear. For fear impoverishes always, while sorrow may enrich.
>
> Kumalo looked at him, with an intensity of gaze that was strange in so humble a man, and hard to encounter.
>
> —I do not know that I am enriched, he said.
>
> —Sorrow is better than fear, said Father Vincent. Fear is a journey, a terrible journey, but sorrow is at least an arriving.
>
> —And where have I arrived, asked Kumalo.
>
> —When the storm threatens, a man is afraid for his house, said Fr. Vincent in that symbolic language that is like the Zulu tongue. But when the house is destroyed, there is something to do. About the storm he can do nothing, but he can rebuild a house.[14]

I've always believed that when a story follows you through life, not allowing you to forget it, there's some guidance abiding in its pages. Something is calling to you, perhaps wanting to help you remember something too precious to forget.

Alan Paton's *Too Late the Phalarope* also has me under its spell. It reads like poetic prose. I will never forget the unforgettable characters I met in this book. It is the story of a young white South African police officer who is greatly loved, almost idolized in his community. When he violates one of the strictest laws of his country concerning relationship between black and white, it is heartwarming to see who stands beside him to the end. It is a spellbinding portrayal of inner struggle, compassion, and forgiveness! The following quote from *Phalarope* lingers in my memory: "There's a hard law that when a deep injury has been done to us, we never recover until we forgive."[15]

❧   Is there an experience of forgiveness that lives on as a good memory in your life?

❧   What are your memories of rebuilding your house after a spiritual storm?

❧   What are your good memories of tears?

THE SIGN OF JONAS

Thomas Merton has been one of the most significant authors of my life. He is a monastic companion on my journey, a brother, and a friend. I have probably spent more time in communion with him in prayer than with any other contemporary saint. Although I did not enter monastic life because of him, his writings were instrumental in my perseverance. For this reason I have always had an endearing and enduring bond with this lovable and perplexing monk. The pages of his journals portray a lover and a questioner. His passion for God, his quest for the truth, his restless seeking heart and hunger for justice, his humor: all these pieces of his personality have drawn me to him. He has been one of the most important spiritual guides for my life.

I reread *The Sign of Jonas* when I was going through a lot of inner turmoil and questioning, fighting a seemingly unending battle with authority both in the church and in community. It was a few years after I had made my final monastic vows. *The Sign of Jonas* was a turning point for me. I have vivid memories of reading it on a summer day in July at my favorite rock table on our monastery grounds. For some reason the tenderness of Merton's questions softened my warring spirit. Something gentled in me and I could breathe more easily. Hope moved in again. That July morning lives on in my memory as does this beautiful passage taken from his well known "Fire-Watch" essay toward the end of the book:

> And now my whole being breathes the wind which blows through the belfry, and my hand is on the door through which I see the heavens. The door swings out

upon a vast sea of darkness and of prayer. Will it come like this, the moment of my death? Will You open a door upon the great forest and set my feet upon a ladder under the moon, and take me out among the stars?

I lay the clock upon the belfry ledge and pray cross-legged with my back against the tower, and face the same unanswered questions.

Lord God of this great night: do You see the woods? Do You hear the rumor of their loneliness? Do You behold their secrecy? Do You remember their solitudes? Do You see that my soul is beginning to dissolve like wax within me?

Do You remember the place by the stream? . . . Do You remember the time of the forest fire? Do You know what has become of the little poplars we planted in the spring? Do You observe the valley where I marked the trees?

There is no leaf that is not in Your care. There is no cry that was not heard by You before it was uttered. There is no water in the shales that was not hidden there by Your wisdom. There is no concealed spring that was not concealed by You.

. . . There is greater comfort in the substance of silence than in the answer to a question. Eternity is in the present. Eternity is in the palm of the hand. Eternity is a seed of fire, whose sudden roots break barriers that keep my heart from being an abyss.

The things of time are in connivance with eternity. The shadows serve You. The beasts sing to You before they pass away. The solid hills shall vanish like a worn-out garment. All things change, and die and disappear. Questions arrive, assume their actuality, and also disappear. In this hour I shall cease to ask them, and silence shall be my answer.

. . . You, who sleep in my breast, are not met with words, but in the emergence of life within life and of wisdom within wisdom. You are found in communion. . . .[16]

Reading this now, it seems that Merton himself is musing on the gold in his memories. There is gold in our questions and we ought not be afraid to ask them. However, the answers to our questions live somewhere in the silence of our lives until, as the poet Rilke suggests, we live our way into the answer.

❧ If you were to choose a spiritual guide from among the many authors you've read, who would you choose?

❧ Recall an author who ministered to you at a very low time in your life.

❧ Read again the quote from Merton's "Fire-Watch" essay. Write your own intimate conversation with God.

The Perfection of the Morning

For some of us there may come a time when we are called to go on a journey through the desert of our lives, a journey of the soul. Sharon Butala has crafted a classic work of art in this lovely memoir, *The Perfection of the Morning*. She explains that she couldn't go on trying to find a new life for herself after her divorce until she had some clarity about her old life. Her journey took her to places in her spirit where she had never been. She ventured into a new land geographically and into a new relationship with the earth and with herself. While embracing the newness of so many things she was forced to also examine the old.

Some of us go through the painful journey that involves the severing of bonds. Whether the severing takes place in the dissolving of a marriage, a long-term relationship, a ministry or profession, a promised life of commitment in a religious community or priesthood, there is pain involved. There is a kind of divorce or separation. Sometimes this estrangement may take place in the area of our faith. We are led into new ways of believing and processing life. This too can be painful. I believe that all separations invite us to go on a journey that feels like death, but can in reality be the beginning of new life.

We don't have to make that journey. We can remain in a relationship, but live as though we're divorced. We can live in a community of monastics, but not really be there in spirit. The body may be where the heart is not. In an attempt to live a more wholesome life, we can choose to do a piece of life-work that may or may not take us out of our present situation. In either case, some kind of journey of the soul is essential.

Sharon Butala describes her experience as a wilderness journey in which she was called to examine and revisit her experience of being woman. She writes:

> Women experience the world differently than men do. . . .
> If left alone to try it, we would live it differently . . . we
> haven't yet told our stories out of the fullness and
> uniqueness of our femininity. . . . Until we tell the truth
> out loud, no matter how humiliating or painful or at
> variance with society's version, we will not come to
> know what we are, what is truly our world of experi-
> ence, and through that, what our roles should be, what
> we can be. . . .
> That was one result of my long sojourn in the
> metaphorical wilderness. I began to believe I had to
> write out of that deep, abandoned, forgotten, ignored
> and discredited place in myself where surely I would
> find what there was in me that was wholly woman. I
> thought, the only way to find out what a woman is and
> might be is to speak only the truth out of one's own feel-
> ings. . . . I wanted to cut away what I had been taught, I
> wanted to shut my eyes and close my ears and my door
> and only write from the deepest part of myself, to say
> how things seem to me, what I honestly feel before
> thought, about the world and my experience in it.[17]

This is a book I want to read more than once. It nestles in my memory like a new friend. It was kind of a vision quest for me. I started missing the author and her courageous spiritual struggle the moment I closed the book. My spirit lifts as I hear her assert that no one will ever again tell her what she thinks. I pray a quiet amen as I move along on my own wilderness journey.

❧ Has there been a divorce or severing of bonds in your life that has taught you wisdom and brought you to new places of growth?

❧ Reflect on an important life experience in which you discovered yourself anew.

THE MUSIC OF SILENCE

Sometimes in reading a book I find myself spontaneously saying, "Oh, I wish I had written this book." David Steindl-Rast's *The Music of Silence* is such a book for me. In his quiet, poetic way he journeys with us through the hours of the monastic day from the night-watch of early morning Vigils to the Great Silence of the night prayer Compline. This book is fashioned in such a way so as to encourage us not only to say the words of the psalms, but to reflect on the special virtue of each hour. In doing this we create a contemplative presence as we live our lives around these hours.

For some reason this lovely work stirs up in me memories of my life as a young monastic. I hear again the call to step out of "clock time" and be present to the sacredness of each moment. At one point, as I was praying with this lovely work, I was led to remember a time when I was perhaps more fervent and my vocation was new and fresh. I was reminded of a text from the Christian scriptures: " . . . you have turned aside from your early love" (Revelation 2:4). This reminder invited me to review my life in terms of being in love and living in love. Memories of my early love were good memories. I am confident this love still abides. It waits within me to be awakened and rediscovered. *The Music of Silence* helped me to connect with my early love in monastic life.

Although I have always struggled with schedules and structure, the rhythm of the monastic life keeps bringing me back to what is essential. I am discovering that one can be on a schedule without being a slave to the schedule and without being rigid. The burning question for me these days is, "Am I free enough to hear the invitation of each moment?" If I'm slavishly attached to the previous moment, or if I'm already living tomorrow's moments, then I am not free for the moment of the eternal now. Thus it will slip away without me.

Reflecting on the well loved hour of Vespers, David writes,

> Vespers is the hour that invites peace of heart, which is the reconciling of contradictions within ourselves and around us. Rilke has a beautiful poem in *The Book of Hours* in which he speaks of someone who makes peace among his life's many contradictions. It defies translation, but I will paraphrase it here.
>
> "Whoever gathers his life's many contradictions into one, gratefully makes of them a single symbol, expels all the noisy ones from his palace and becomes in a new way festive. Then you, God, are the guest whom he receives in gentle evening hours. You are the second to his solitude, the quiet center of his monologues, and every time he circles around you, you stretch his compass beyond time."
>
> Within time, again, we receive that which goes beyond time. Within this evening hour, when we become festive in a new way and receive God as a guest, we stretch that compass of time beyond and embrace the now. That's the serenity, the peace of heart, the ability to embrace the inevitable contradictions the day leaves behind, which is the mood of Vespers.[18]

Having read *The Music of Silence*, I am trying to be more attentive to the virtue of each hour. I find myself longing to dwell in the eternal now. These special times of prayer, the hours of the office, are like bookmarks. They help me keep my place along the way.

❦ Make a special effort this week to be attentive to important moments of each day: pre-dawn, sunrise, mid-morning, noon, mid-afternoon, sunset (the Vespers hour), and night-time. Write your own prayer for these special times and make plans for a day of retreat so as to be able to live these times more attentively.

GLITTERING IMAGES ...

When I finished reading Susan Howatch's brilliant and inspiring *Church of England* series, I honestly didn't know how I could live without her characters in my life. Melding a combination of psychology, theology, spirituality, and mysticism, she companions her fascinating characters on their faith journeys, portraying a remarkable understanding of human nature. These amazing mystery stories of the soul have a therapeutic effect on me. They are filled with unforgettable personalities, flawed and fragile, intelligent and foolish, lovable and loving, believing and doubting, searching, forgiving, challenging, controlling, and exasperating. Howatch fashions characters I can believe in.

Each book can stand on its own but, in my opinion, it is best to read them in the order they were written. Each new book will be like picking up on the life story of old friends. The order of the series is as follows: *Glittering Images, Glamorous Powers, Ultimate Prizes, Scandalous Risks, Mystical Paths,* and *Absolute Truths*.

A conversation toward the end of *Scandalous Risks* will give you a brief introduction to one of my favorite characters. Lovable Venetia is full of passion and bad judgments. I hope she is at peace finally. In talking with one of the leading characters, she begins the conversation:

> "I know I've made a complete and utter mess of my life, but it's far too late now to start all over again!"
>
> "It's never too late. . . . It's always possible to rise from the grave of pain, alienation and despair."
>
> "Even when one's buried beneath a concrete slab."

"Yes! . . . Even then!"

"But how do I achieve this resurrection? Go back to the Church?"

At once he became somber. "I know the Church has failed you. The Church is as fallible and imperfect as the men who run it, and I could never blame you . . . if you hold the Church in contempt. But if you could look past the Church now to the eternal truths which lie beyond."

" . . . But how do I connect with them, how do I tune in, how do I dial their number?"

"They're not at the end of a telephone line. They're waiting on your doorstep, and all you have to do is open the great closed door, the door that Holman Hunt painted, the door that has to be opened from within."

. . . Then I astonished myself by saying: "I can picture Christ standing at the great closed door. But I can't see myself on the inside. I think I'm on the outside, watching him, and beyond the door is my new resurrected life, but I can't figure out how to get there. So it's no good Christ just standing by the door with his lamp. That's too passive. He's got to act, he's got to stretch out his hand and grab me so that he can heave me over the threshold."[19]

I suspect Christ has to do that for many of us. Who says the door can only be opened from the inside? What is there to prevent Christ from stepping right through the locked doors of our hearts and making a home in us without our consent? Perhaps when this happens, transformation can begin.

🌿 Sometimes we are called to solve the mystery behind the mystery of our lives, e.g., Why are we behaving so abominably? What is the underlying cause of all the bad judgments we make? Why do we end up doing the things we don't want to do? Why must we dominate and control? Reflect on these questions and the mystery of your life.

A PRAYER FOR OWEN MEANY

I am going to say very little about this novel because in many ways it is so bizarre that you might wonder why on earth I am featuring it in this chapter. Yet of all the characters I've ever met in a novel, I have missed Owen Meany the most. In many ways it is—how shall I say this?—a tastefully irreverent book. If you read it with an open mind, however, you will find much wisdom hidden in the lives of Owen and his friend John who is telling the story.

Perhaps the reason I loved it so much is because it created so many moods in me. At times I would laugh until tears rolled down my cheeks. At other times I found myself weeping. Then there were those moments when I was drawn to lay the book aside and meditate, to ask my own questions about faith, to pray for our country and our church, to search out memories of my roots.

This book will linger in my life forever. I can't forget Owen Meany—his voice, his size, his faith, his strange fate and destiny. I even own a sweatshirt that says, "I Miss Owen Meany."

The first paragraph of the book won me over and made me a disciple forever:

> I am doomed to remember a boy with a wrecked voice, not because of his voice, or because he was the smallest person I ever knew, or even because he was the instrument of my mother's death, but because he is the reason I believe in God; I am a Christian today because of Owen Meany.[20]

Although I wouldn't put this novel in the profound category that I find myself placing Bryce Courtney's *The Power of One*, for reasons that defy my understanding, it remains forever in my heart—my all-time favorite novel.

I miss Owen Meany.

❧ Spend some time remembering your favorite characters from books you've read.

❧ Which characters do you miss the most? What is it about them that affects you and will not let them exit your memory?

An Accidental Monk

This charming little book is probably no longer in print. It found me long ago in one of those moments when I was struggling with eternal questions. It is written by Marylee Mitcham who in the 70s felt a call to strip away all but the necessities of life and to live simply and prayerfully. In the following quote, the call to her accidental vocation to simplicity and prayer is described.

> I have come upon my religious life like one comes upon a clearing in the woods. The grace of God has given me space and a cottage to set up housekeeping and the grace of God slowly provides me with the simple accouterments I need to live. . . .
> *It is a terrible thing to fall into the hands of the living God!*
> . . . I am a writer on kitchen walls; and for two years those words have lived on my wall and in my heart. I have been in the Church six years now and I have come to know a little of her riches. It astounds me to enter at a time when others are leaving. I do not understand. . . . I concentrate on the small, on what unfolds in my way within the Way. I am merely a wife, a friend to some, and an accidental monk.
> I have received a call to my accidental vocation . . . I know I have received it because I experience the grace that flows from my struggle to answer that call . . . the struggle itself is never consoling; it always feels hard and lonely and beyond me. I could say it this way: my consent feels like leaving home; God's grace feels like

coming home; the struggle to be faithful to a call feels like being outside in the weather.[21]

I came upon this book at a time when I was struggling to be faithful to my call to simplicity and prayer and these words encouraged me. Here was a woman who was not a vowed religious filled with a burning desire to adopt certain aspects of monastic life, especially simplicity and unceasing prayer.

It was penance that drew her into the Church, she said, because she knew how to cooperate with death better than life. As I read this book again today I am moved to prayer at that remark. In my early monastic life I felt quite drawn to detachment. It is as though I, too, knew how to cooperate with death better than life. Today I find myself leaning toward the life I never lived. It is not that I have stopped believing that detachment is of value. But I have grown into believing that I must be attached to things and people in a healthy kind of way, or perhaps I could say I must be attached with a certain amount of detachment.

Her prayer, says Marylee, consists in remembering who she is. The simplicity of her words startles me with longing, "As far as I can see, prayer is the only means for me to be myself. Until I learn to pray unceasingly, I won't act like who I am."[22]

❦ When Marylee Mitcham says she is an *accidental monk* she means, of course, that although she is not a vowed monastic living in community, she feels called to live the gospel in the radical way a monk is called. Could such a call become a reality in your life? Can you remember a time when you longed for greater simplicity?

❦ How do you react to her statement that prayer is the only way to be yourself?

❦ There is nothing universally great about this small book, I suppose; yet it is a book I've not forgotten. That's what makes it great for me. What are the books that live on in your memory? Which books would you like to read a second time? In books you have read who are some of the unforgettable characters that linger in your mind and heart?

THE DANCE OF THE DISSIDENT DAUGHTER

The title of this book intrigues me. There has always been a fair amount of dissidence in my life, and in reading Sue Monk Kidd's book I began to realize that my dissidence has a certain integrity about it. The dissidence I so often feel is, in reality, an obedience to my native feminine soul. I have been grateful for the dance of many obedient dissident daughters. I think it is time for me to dance with them.

This book has had a powerful effect on me. The author openly and creatively tells the story of her growing awareness of the sin of patriarchy and her awakening to the sacred feminine. She moves on a courageous journey through initiation, grounding, and empowerment. There is no place so alive, she says, as on the edge of becoming.

In ways both frightening and challenging, this book is helping me to find my own voice. In her wise, insightful style Sue Monk Kidd encourages me on my quest:

> Forming an honest feminist critique of our own faith tradition is not an easy thing to do. Betrayal of any kind is hard, but betrayal by one's religion is excruciating. It makes you want to rage and weep. It deposits a powerful energy inside.
>
> Eventually that energy will flow out as either hostility or love. The energy must and will find a form, a shape, in our lives. It is now, as we wade into the secret distress of the feminine and encounter the largeness of the wound, that we need to be very conscious and keep the despair we might feel from becoming channeled into bitterness. We have to work very hard to keep it flowing toward compassion.[23]

❧ What is your experience of juggling compassion and bitterness?

❧ Do you recall a *dissident* moment that was in reality an *obedient* moment?

❧ Have you felt the excitement of being *on the edge of becoming?*

❧ This is a book that might stretch you. Consider reading it with an open heart.

BRIDGE ACROSS MY SORROWS

Christina Noble's heart-rending memoir is a testament to the truth that there is within each of us "that which can never die." One reviewer described the book as "a record of grief and courage that would take a tear from a stone." I read Christina's story with a flood of emotions. She grew up in Dublin, Ireland, in the midst of unspeakable poverty, abuse, and neglect. During her years of living as a street child, and later in an abusive marriage, we see an indomitable spirit that keeps reaching for life. It is difficult to fathom a person experiencing such overwhelming terror and still being able to see beauty.

In 1971 she had a dream in which naked children were running down a dirt road fleeing from a napalm bombing. The ground under the children was breaking and the children were reaching out to her for protection. Above the fleeing children a brilliant white light contained the word "Vietnam." This dream-vision lingered in her soul. It guided her to find a way to build a bridge across her sorrows. It summoned her to work among the *bui doi,* the street children of Vietnam. She, who was once a street child herself, heard their cry for love. Perhaps because her memories were not golden memories, she chose a life of helping those with fearful memories to make new memories. She herself is the *gold* who came through all her painful memories—scarred and beautiful.

She claims that when reporters come and see her work in Vietnam they repeatedly refer to her as a Mother Teresa. About that, however, she has this to say,

I belt out songs in clubs, songs about strong feelings and anger. I shout about the rights of children. I enjoy a double whiskey now and then. I love dancing. I like to ride fast on the back of a Honda. . . . I detest violence but if I have to protect a child by giving someone a wallop, I'll do it! I'm more than a little bit wild. I'm Irish. Mother Teresa I am not.

. . . The child is the lifeline of the world. We can talk forever about the ozone layer and about the environment, but what good is a clean environment if the inhabitants of the world are thugs? A child learns from its elders. If a child is kicked from the womb on to the street, all it knows is segregation and selfishness.

When I first came to Vietnam I was afraid. I didn't want to feel any more pain. I knew that day in the park if I touched those two little girls that I was in this thing for the rest of my life. And I knew even then it was not going to be easy: I had no money, no education, no business connections . . . I had nothing. . . . I was nobody. . . . When I began here in Vietnam, people said what I wanted to do was impossible. "You are only one person," they said. But when I was a child, I needed only one person to love me. One is very important.[24]

LET BEAUTY IN

When I periodically sort through my books, trying to diminish my supply and gain greater simplicity, these are some of the books I cannot bear to part with. They would not have to remain in my possession to live on in my memory. Yet I find them comforting, as though the message they contain is still calling quietly for me to listen . . . "Listen," an old proverb teaches, "Listen or your tongue will keep you deaf." I keep trying to listen to the wisdom these books have offered me.

On other days I read the book of silence. For no words, no matter how lovely they may be, hold much meaning until they are finally eaten in silence.

A few people may show surprise that the books I listed here are not necessarily religious books. To that I can only say that while they may not be religious in the traditional under- standing of religious, I hold that all of these books are deeply spiritual. They have all helped me to be more myself, thus, they have helped me to pray.

Just as I have listed books that have inspired me and taught me wisdom, we could do the same with pieces of mu- sic, art, and drama. So much beauty lingers in our memory. Let's learn to call it home. On difficult days it can be comfort- ing to return to some lovely piece of art, or a character in a book or film. Invite these treasures to bless you again. You may be amazed at the magic they can still bring about in your life. Let beauty in.

A Meditation for Authors and Readers

In the beginning was God's word
and the word was beautiful.
The word was good.
And the word exploded
into billions and billions of words.
Then God created authors
to mold and shape
and give new meanings to the words.
The authors, who were themselves God's word,
gathered up the words
and flung them out into the space of the universe
and into the space and galaxies of their souls.

And the word became poetry.
The word became essays and stories,
journals and memoirs
and newspapers.
The word became history.
And the word became joy and sorrow,
pain and peace.

The word became challenging,
comforting and frightening.
The word became loving, delightful, and humorous.
The word became angry and full of anguish.
And the word was still good.

And then God sent readers
with curious, creative, seeking minds
and open, hungry, probing, questioning hearts.
As they eagerly devoured the words
they became receivers of the Word.
Some of the words fell so freely
into those open hearts
that the great Word of Silence
was needed
to fathom the depths
of the original Word.

Faithful Artist of the ages, In the beginning was the Word. You summoned the Word to become dynamic in our lives. Thank you for gifting us with authors, sowers, and servants of your words. Bless those who gather up your words, refashioning them to tell a story—those who give new life to old words enabling them to touch hearts, to heal, to draw forth tears and laughter, to call forth memories.

May the authors we cherish be blessed and renewed through their writing. Teach them how to be ministers of your original Word, born on the first day of creation. We pray for all authors as they struggle to be ministers of the Word. O God, be with them in their untiring efforts to be a creative force in our world:

May they find inspiration and imagination in their daily lives.

May they be seekers of truth.

May they be given the wisdom of waiting before an empty page.

May their writing be a ministry as well as a profession.

May they stretch minds and open hearts.

May the hard work of writing be a challenge rather than a discouragement.

Source of Life, you who have written your Word in the fiber of our beings, bless deeply and fruitfully all authors. Teach them to dwell and abide with the Word, so that the fruit of their abiding might become a gift for readers.

Thank you for readers who appreciate words and see in them symbols of revelation. Give us good books and hungry minds. Instill in each of us a desire for truth. Send words that will heal our planet, words that will become flesh in our lives, giving us the courage and vision to build a new creation.

Lead authors and readers together to hunger for the wisdom that comes from you. This we ask of you who are the Author of All Life.

EXERCISES

1. In your journal list five books that are *golden* in your memory. Beside each book you've listed write a few words that sums up why this book lives on in your memory.

2. Books, including fiction, can be a marvelous means of spiritual enrichment. Write a letter to one of your favorite book characters. Allow yourself to be vulnerable in the letter.

3. Make plans to read one of the books that I've described in this chapter.

> When I get a little money
> I buy books,
> And if any is left
> I buy food and clothing
> —Erasmus

4. Recommend a book to someone this week.

FINDING YOUR WAY TO THE GOLD: THE PATH OF RITUAL

*Something is waiting for us
to make ground for it.
Something that lingers near us,
something that loves,
something that waits
for the right ground to be made
so it can make its full presence known.*

—Clarissa Pinkola Estes
The Faithful Gardener

So how do we find our way to the gold when there is no rainbow in sight?

The path of ritual can lead us there. Within us is a natural tendency to act out our soul's deepest feelings and questions. From ancient times to the present we have searched for ways to honor and name the sacred within us and around us, and to glorify the Divine Source from whom all things come. Continually we seek out new ways to ritualize our relationship with the environment, one another, and God.

Ritual is a way of celebrating who we are. It is also an attempt to touch who we've been and who we're becoming. When we want to honor the soul's deepest longings and leanings, we devise rituals to help us find our way home. As Clarissa Pinkola Estes says so beautifully in our opening quote, there is something in us that wants to make its full presence known.[1] That which is waiting to make its full presence known is the *hidden gold* in us. When I speak here of "the gold," I'm referring to the truth of our lives with all its joyful, painful, and beautiful stories. Even the pain is edged in gold because it is part of the texture of our lives. It has helped to shape us into the persons we are today. On some of our ritual journeys we may discover pieces of forgiveness we never dreamed we possessed. In the deep ground of our being we will find incredible power and strength ready to be mined. We will encounter love, hope, and faith, all waiting to make their full presence known.

In this chapter I will be sharing with you some of the rituals that have helped me discover missing pieces of the mosaic of my life. These missing pieces are things like lost joy, the ability to forgive, living in the present moment, memory of significant people, the healing aspect of grief, ways to befriend my fears, knowing my roots, et cetera.

A ritual does not have to be a complex, elaborate formula of prayer. It can be as simple as a one-line chant or a gesture of blessing. It might be a poem or a letter in which you give voice to the *presence* that waits to make itself known. Or, it could be a dance or song through which you express your feelings. It may be a pilgrimage to a historic place or to a gravesite.

It could also be a silent standing in attention, a quiet way of honoring some hallowed memory from the past.

I have discovered that returning to *beginning places* can be immensely healing. These places might include the site of your conception or birth, baptismal fonts, playgrounds, your church or childhood school, the house or land where you grew up, your first job, your old high school, the place where you were married. . . . At these *beginning places* you can create your own rituals, sing your own songs, and touch again *the gold in your memories*. Sometimes memories of pain will accompany you on these pilgrimages. You may begin to understand just how far you have come on your journey. Perhaps the faces of wise guides who have walked with you through some of life's difficult moments will rise before you like light in the darkness. If possible, offer hospitality to all of your memories. Memories are pathways to moments that have become eternal. John O'Donohue says this so well in his book, *Anam Cara*:

> Time as the rhythm of soul has an eternal dimension where everything is gathered and minded. Here nothing is lost. This is a great consolation: The happenings in your life do not disappear. Nothing is ever lost or forgotten. Everything is stored within your soul in the temple of memory. Therefore, as an old person, you can happily go back and attend to your past time; you can return through the rooms of that temple, visit the days that you enjoyed and the times of difficulty where you grew and refined yourself.[2]

RITUALS OF BIRTH AND DEATH

We often miss opportunities for ritual celebrations because we fail to realize that in addition to the ceremonies we hold in our churches, we also need to bring rituals into our homes. In a way, the home is the primary church. The parents, or caregivers, are the priests and priestesses of the household. Can you imagine the intimate impact on the family if, when a new child is brought home, there would be a ritual of reception and welcome in the home?

Try to envision family and friends gathered in a circle. The child is lovingly passed around the circle for each person to hold and bless. A prayer of well-wishing is offered as you bless this new little person.

> May you be happy.
> May you be wise.
> May you grow strong and healthy in all ways.
> May something good happen to you every day.
> May you always walk with God.
> May you be clothed with the virtues of faith, hope, and
>   love.
> May Jesus be a companion on your way.
> May you find joy in little things.
> May tears be welcomed in your life.
> May you remember your divine origin.
> May you be open to the secrets in your soul.

Stories are told of the aboriginal peoples reverently holding a new child up to the heavens. What a wonderful way of helping the child to have good memories!

One of the rituals that I've made a part of my life is the celebration of my birthday once a month. I used to make plans for a retreat day every month but seldom kept my good intention. I needed to find a way to help me remember to do this on a monthly basis so I chose the day of my birth. On the twenty-eighth of every month I make a special effort to spend more time in prayer, to have a greater awareness of others, to spend some time with beauty, to reflect gratefully on my birth. It is a celebration of what is most important in life. Even when I'm traveling and can't take a day off, I still find ways to make this day unique. For me, it's not a day to receive presents. It's a day to be present. I also try to give a little gift to someone on this day.

One of the things I've added to my monthly birthday is the ritual of praying for my family, community, special friends, and mentors who have contributed to my ongoing spiritual birth. I purchased a small photograph album, the kind that holds just one photo on each page. It has become a prayer book for me. On the twenty-eighth of each month I page through it slowly, connecting gratefully with those people who are part of the gold in my memories. These simple patterns in my schedule call me to be attentive to treasures I might otherwise take for granted.

Once on my monthly birthday I spent a good portion of the day in my childhood forest. I took with me only a book of children's poems, my journal, and a banana. The banana was a reminder of a favorite treat Mama used to bring home for me once in awhile when she went to get groceries. Now in my adult years, with a clearer understanding of just how frugal our budget was in those days, the memory of the banana is more cherished than ever. From the book of poems I prayed with two of my childhood favorites, "I Have a Little Shadow," and "The Swing," both by Robert Louis Stevenson.

This day in the forest turned out to be a kind of natural ritual. There was nothing planned. It was a very simple day of walking through the woods, leaning against the trees, sitting in the trees, gathering acorns. I sat in the dry creekbed where I once loved to play with my sisters, brothers, and cousins. Closing my eyes and journeying back in time I could hear again the voices of children playing. I read my poems, ate my banana slowly, and remembered. . . . It was a very happy birthday. Upon leaving the forest I scribbled a few lines in my journal:

> What is the value of this remembering? Does it add anything to my life?
>
> Yes! I think it does. In my old forest I touched the past today. So many things I thought had died, but they only changed form. They wear the shape of mystery now. A new awareness, like the morning sun, has risen in my soul. I walk from the forest awake.

I am aware that the spirits of my ancestors linger here, and depart with me as well. What I sometimes call heaven is all around me. I walk with a sweet loneliness away from the forest, one hand grasping birth, the other death. A new vision of life has been the gift of this day. I have lived one day in the heart of the forest with mindfulness and utter presence. What I thought had died has come to life.

I went to the forest to find my way to the gold. Memories of life and death danced with me under the trees. Birth and death, like joy and sorrow, are companions on all our ritual journeys. Although it was birth I was contemplating on that day, a little death crept in as well.

Rituals of birth and death can be enriching. While birth is ordinarily a time of joy, death is usually difficult. We are left with memories: sometimes guilt and anger, immense grief, often loneliness. On occasion we may be fortunate enough to experience the consolation that comes when, with a circle of family and friends, we are able to gather around the bedside of a dying loved one, exchange words of gratitude, and say good-bye.

MAMA AND PAPA

In my personal life I've never experienced the consolation of a tender bedside farewell. My mother died quite suddenly when I was twenty-three years old. A great sadness in my life is that she died before I had matured enough to have the kind of relationship with her that I now long to have had. I can say the same of my father. He died a year later, partially of a broken heart.

When my mother died I never took the time to grieve for her. All my sorrow went out to my father. His sadness laid on my heart like a brick. When he died I felt a certain sense of relief that he was being set free from the weight of his loneliness. Thus, I didn't take sufficient time to grieve for him either. Only now do I realize how important it is to take time for grief.

We all work out our grief in different ways. When the four most significant people in my life died, something happened to me. It was as though I checked out, almost as if I left my body until life got back to normal. I was present, going through the motions of weeping, of comforting others, and receiving comfort myself, but in another sense I wasn't there.

Mourning is a very solitary rite for me; for some reason I have to go through it alone. I can be there with my family members and friends, saying all the right things. But after the funeral is over, after the guests have gone, after I have returned to the life I'm trying to live, I begin making plans to celebrate my grief. I search out a place of retreat, a space where I can be alone with my memories and ritualize all this person has been for me. Sometimes the ritual takes place shortly after the death; but there are times when I have waited as long as twenty-five years or more.

I waited a long time to ritualize my parents' deaths. When I finally took the time to do so it was like shedding a great burden. I had no idea so much stuff was stored in my heart and soul. I chose to go to *Hesychia*, our community house of prayer, just an hour away from the place where I was born. It is a beautiful spot surrounded by hills, woods, and meadows. I spent three days there. One day was spent with my mother. The next day I journeyed with my father. The last day was a summary day for myself and a visit to my old church and to the gravesite of my parents.

There was no structured ritual planned for this time of prayerful entering into my memories. I was simply giving myself the time to feel whatever needed to be felt. I had taken with me photos and other tangible mementos to pray and ponder. My time was spent in remembering, loving, thanking, weeping, forgiving. I talked to my parents and wrote them letters. I took walks with them. I journaled. I sang songs. I sat quietly allowing myself to feel the sorrows and joys of their lives and mine.

My grief was edged in gold. This was a valuable discovery for me. I felt immensely fortunate to be able to feel so deeply and weep so freely. I know people who would pay all

the gold in the world to own a few of my tears. Weeping in itself can be a healing ritual—an immense release. Not to be able
to cry is a great burden.

When we do grief work it is usually more than that final
letting go that we are grieving. So often there are memories of
relationships we never had, things we never got around to saying to one another. In my opinion it is never too late to say
what is in our hearts. Say it. And be at peace.

And so, on those cold January days, in the privacy of my
hermitage I said what I needed to say to my parents. I share
with you an excerpt from each of my letters:

Mama,

The evening sun is setting over the winter hills. Having spent this day with you, it feels as though you are in
my very soul breathing in me, enfolding me in your presence. As I gaze out into the great space a touching scene
comes into my memory and I am back in time with you.
You are making egg noodles and I'm helping you cut
them out in little strips. I am trying to hurry us along because I want you to go outside to watch the sunset with
me. I have a place already prepared for us. The old picnic quilt is spread out awaiting our arrival. How I loved
watching the sunset with you! It is a poignant memory
now as I watch the sun slip behind the hills. You are so
present I can almost touch you. . . .

My walk with you today has been one of joy and sadness. I know that I must find a way to stop carrying your
sorrow. Your life was so hard. You had such few comforts.
To think about it still almost breaks my heart. The part of
me that longs to fix things wants to reach back in time
and make things different. You seemed so fragile, and I
was terrified that you would be taken away from me.

There was a moment today when it seemed as though
you were saying to me, "My sorrow is now integrated

with all the sorrows and joys of the Body of Christ. Do not let it remain a burden for you. Stand beside someone else and be a loving presence in their sorrow."

. . . A great sadness in my life is that you died before I had matured enough to have a really deep relationship with you. Today I've tried to bond with you—to connect once again in symbolic ways—and I have not been disappointed. I don't know why I waited so long. I hope to stay in touch with you a little more deeply in the future.

. . . Your immense faith in the midst of so much poverty enriches and sustains me to this day. I will always remember the many little ways you brought joy to your children. You remind me of God in your ability to create something out of nothing.

. . . Do you remember the night of the fireflies? The backyards of my soul still glow in remembrance of you.

From a daughter who loves you,

Macrina

Papa,

All day long I called you "Papa." I let that word wash over my soul like a much loved poem, "Papa." I don't know why I ever tried to call you Dad. It just didn't fit, didn't sound right in my mouth. Well, actually I do know why I started calling you Dad. It was because everyone else seemed to be calling their fathers "Dad," and I felt old-fashioned. I wanted to fit in with the crowd, but in my heart it never worked. You will always be Papa to me.

Papa, I don't think I ever really knew you. In a sense you were a strange and private man. It was as though you lived in some other land and I didn't know how to get in to the place where you were. I also think that land was a lonely land and so you drank to fill up the void. . . . I often felt distant from you and even a little fearful. Now in my later years I'm beginning to realize how gifted you were, and I find myself wondering what things would have been like if the opportunity to develop those gifts had been available to you. I remember your beautiful singing voice and the poems you used to write. Only recently I found out that you used to play the violin. I suppose by the time I came along the strings must have been broken and most likely we didn't have the money for repairs. Another recent discovery is that you used to write and direct plays. I'm beginning to realize that a lot of my creativity very likely came from you. That makes me glad because I feel as though I'm moving through life carrying a part of you with me.

Thank you for all those cold winter mornings when you would rise early to build the fire in the wood stove. I remember waking up in our cold room and what a joy it was to find a roaring fire waiting for me in the kitchen. I often smile at the memory of my first sight of snow. You were sitting at the kitchen table having a cup of coffee. As I looked out the window and saw everything white I ran to you calling, "Papa, Papa! Sugar, sugar!"

There was a kind of sadness in my heart today as I prayed with you. It was a nostalgic longing for a relationship that neither of us was capable of having at the time we were given to each other. And yet there was also a warmth and love in my heart, a sense of belonging, a sense of eternity. So as this day ends all is well in my heart. I am your daughter and I love you.

Thanks for the arrowhead. It rests on my altar of prayer, a cherished reminder of you. Whenever I hear someone call their father, "Papa," I feel tender inside and I smile. . . . I keep searching for you and find your spirit searching for me. It is never too late to get to know one another in the spirit. And so we abide.

Your loving daughter,
Macrina

All words limp when I try to describe the healing I experienced on this ritual journey with my mother and father. It was as though a healing prayer had been buried in my being. But the prayer couldn't get out. Finally, my willingness to be present to the pain and joy of my parents' lives gave wings to that prayer. Set free, it flew out of the place where I had imprisoned it, healing not only me, but others as well. There is something in us that wants to pray. And we must learn to listen to that "something" lest we become a graveyard of buried prayers.

Are there any buried prayers in your heart? The world needs them. Let them fly free. One way of freeing your imprisoned prayers is to write down what you're feeling. Be brave. Pack your bags and move back into your house of memories. Allow your feelings and thoughts to flow forth in writing. If you find yourself weeping as you write down these memories, that does not mean there is an absence of gold. Tears can be healing. A memory of beauty can bring forth tears, so, too, can a memory of sorrow. Your tears are part of the gold.

Dorothy

I was only a child when my sister, Dorothy, died. She was seven; I was almost twelve. I knew little about rituals of healing at that time. As a natural part of my life, these rituals did happen although they were totally unplanned and spontaneous, the kind I would like to have restored in my adult life. One of the confusions of my life in those days was that I didn't realize it was possible to be happy and sad at the same time. I didn't know that grief could be edged in gold. So as the days moved into months and the date of Dorothy's death grew further into the past, I would often find myself feeling guilty as I began to feel happy again.

Years later when I was giving a retreat in the Pacific Northwest I had an unexpected experience of healing in a coffee shop. Early one morning I stuffed my journal into my backpack and started walking. Without a goal in mind I was strolling along when suddenly I came upon one of those little espresso coffee shops that are so popular in the northwest. The aroma drew me inside. I decided to treat myself to some special coffee. Sipping my coffee I got out my journal. For some unknown reason Dorothy came to my mind. She was the little girl in the coffin that I referred to in my first chapter. When she died it was still customary in rural communities to bring the body home and keep vigil with it until the burial. Actually, that custom seems much more sacred than gathering in the funeral parlor. Yet as a child it terrified me to have Dorothy in our house when she was not alive. Everyone was saying how beautiful she looked. All I could think about was: What good is it to be beautiful when you are dead? This was a very traumatic experience for me. It was doubly traumatic because she and I had had a small quarrel the morning she left for the hospital. I wouldn't look at her when she waved good-bye. My heart was broken in ways I could not explain to my family. I never talked about that.

And so on this early May morning, she came into my memory bright as a star. I remembered the spontaneous ritual that freely flowed out of my child-spirit a few months after her death. It began under a pine tree and ended with a dance in the tall meadow grass, a place where we used to dance together. It was really a kind of mystical moment, but I was too young to name it at the time.

That memory returned to my consciousness as I sat journaling in a little coffee shop in Olympia, Washington. There was gold in the memory. Harvesting that childhood moment filled me with gratitude, awe, and delight. I allowed my thoughts to flow like a river. Here is a piece of what I wrote that day.

Joy and sorrow are sisters,
they live in the same house.

Dorothy and I were sisters,
living in the same house.
She walked out one morning
just before my twelfth birthday,
never to return again.

Then the life in me began to fade,
growing dimmer and dimmer
until I was gasping for breath.
Some strange monster
was stuck in my throat.
It's name was sorrow.

It crept through my household,
an unwelcome guest.
And everyone in our house
had breathing problems,
for the monster had hold of us all.
But we never talked about it
because we didn't know how.

In those days I didn't know,
that if you welcomed the monster
by taking its hand, and
inviting it into your life,
it would be transformed into
a lover and a friend.

Then one day, way down
in the bottom of my heart,
Sorrow's sister, Joy,

---

started humming songs of life,
coaxing me out of my lifelessness.

She set my feet a'dancing.
I was dancing on the edge of sorrow,
dancing on the edge of joy.
Sorrow holding on to one hand,
Joy hopefully gripping the other.
These are the sisters who carried me through
the trauma of my first death.

Now the monster has gone away
to torment the unenlightened.
A sad, sweet sorrow remains
and it never sends joy away,
ever since that day
when Dorothy returned
to teach me:
Joy and sorrow are sisters;
they live in the same house.

It was a gloriously quiet morning. The customers were
mostly drive-through which suited me just fine and gave me a
sense of privacy, for as I wrote the tears came. The healing moment from which this poem flowed took place a few months
after Dorothy's death.[3] Unexpectedly, in my adult life, I was
suddenly able to put words to the experience. Life gives us
those opportunities as we learn to be open to the voiceless
sounds surrounding us. Perhaps there is a poem in you waiting to make its full presence known.

THE WILD MAN OF GOD

One last piece of personal grief work I want to share with
you concerns John, the priest who was a mentor to me in my
early years as a monastic. Although I had been to his funeral,
something seemed missing. I longed for the opportunity to

make a pilgrimage to his grave. I wanted to stand there *alone*. For me, there is something intimate and sacred about solitary moments of grief. No one can do my grief work for me. All the kind words offered fall on my closed ears until I've done a certain piece of processing the grief myself.

I knew I needed to stand by John's grave, remembering. I wanted to remember again his humor and joy, his free spirit, his love of ritual, his passionate belief that rigidity and rules are not what is most important in the church, his persistent effort to make God real in people's lives.

One day while driving home from Oklahoma City I realized that I was very close to the abbey where he was buried. Spontaneously, I was drawn to make my desired pilgrimage. At one point I stopped the car, climbed over a fence, and started gathering wildflowers. I arrived at his grave with an offering of Black-eyed Susans, purple thistles, and some other lovely weeds whose names I didn't know. This seemed the perfect gift for the wild man of God. Anything from the floral shop would have been far too tame.

Much to my surprise, a red rose lay on his grave. I stared at that rose unbelievingly. Someone had been there not long before. The rose was fresh. I sat down on the grave full of feelings. How I wished that rose might have been placed there by one of his brother monks. I doubt that it was. Most likely it was from someone from the parish church where he had been pastor before he died. I placed my wildflowers beside the rose.

Dear John,

. . . Thank you for believing in me when I had no idea of my gifts.

Thank you for the risks you took to teach what you believed. Thanks for opening the door for women to serve at the altar and break open the Word of God even back in the 60s. Thanks for your holy disobedience. Thank you for encouraging me to ask questions and for enabling me to stay open to change. In my gift of wildflowers I'm trying to tell you that I miss your wild spirit more than I can say.

But now that I see the rose lying here I have to say, "There was a rose in you too!" Those of us who loved you saw even that side of yourself that wasn't readily visible. I will try to keep your spirit alive in my heart.

OFFERINGS AT THE WALL

Some of the most touching stories about people ritualizing the pain, guilt, and anger that come with death can be found in a book entitled *Offerings at the Wall*. The wall is the Vietnam Memorial in Washington, D.C. It has become more than a monument. It is a shrine, a place of pilgrimage where thousands of people come each year to remember those who died in Vietnam. At the wall where the names of the dead are inscribed, people leave offerings of remembrance for their loved ones: touching letters, toys, hats, poetry, boots, flowers, Bibles, teddy bears, photographs, six-packs. . . . Mourners who want to get on with their lives leave these offerings as a memorial of their sadness, rage, loneliness, longing, love. Leaving their gifts at the wall is a healing ritual that helps them connect with their feelings. One of the most heart-rending remembrances offered at the wall, for me, was that of a man who left a photo of a North Vietnamese man and a young girl, along with the following letter.

Dear Sir,

For twenty-two years I have carried your picture in my wallet. I was only eighteen years old that day that we faced one another on that trail in Chu Lai, Vietnam. Why you didn't take my life I'll never know. You stared at me for so long, armed with your AK-47, and yet you did not fire. Forgive me for taking your life, I was reacting the way I was trained, to kill V. C. . . . So many times over the years I have stared at your picture and your daughter, I suspect. Each time my heart and guts would burn with the pain of guilt. I have two daughters myself now. . . . I perceive you as a brave soldier defending his homeland. Above all else, I can now respect the importance that life held for you. I suppose that is why I am here today. . . . It is time for me to continue the life process and release my pain and guilt. Forgive me, Sir.[4]

This is a good example of someone who made a ritual journey to release pain and guilt. Although the memory was not a golden memory, this man must have achieved some kind of peace from this tangible experience at the wall. I cannot stress enough the value of ritualizing the experiences of our lives that are crying out for some kind of release. Sometimes all that is needed is our attentive, loving, and non-judgmental presence to our feelings. It is then we will find the gold.

RITUAL ON 68TH STREET AND 3RD AVENUE, NEW YORK CITY

Leaning against a lamppost on 68th Street in Manhattan, I closed my eyes and tried to travel back in time. "A thousand years, O God," I prayed, "are like yesterday, come and gone, no more than a watch in the night" (Psalm 90:4). It was a brisk October day, the exact date being October 10, 1992. I had come to New York City and to that particular place on a pilgrimage. It was an anniversary ritual. I was trying to touch another day, another year. I was reaching back in time. It was my attempt to connect with a mystery. It is always a little lonely when one is trying to embrace the unembraceable. At such times I try to trust whatever in me is *pure spirit*, that part of me that is most like God. I seek out a place of remembrance of the divine within.

A huge apartment complex was located on the block where I sat in meditation. In my spirit I traveled back ninety-four years to another day. It was October 10, 1899. At that time the New York Foundling Home was on this site. And on this same date in 1899 a young woman with a baby journeyed to the Foundling Home. The woman was my grandmother; the baby was my mother. It must have been a hard journey, yet a journey of love. My grandmother was trying to give her baby a home that, for some unknown reason, she was unable to provide.

I left the lamppost and began to walk slowly around the entire block. I walked in memory of a grandmother and a

grandfather that I never knew. I walked in memory of ancestors I would never know. Arriving back at my original site of
prayer, the lamppost, I sat down again. Taking out a postcard
that I had purchased earlier in the day I felt compelled to write
myself a card as though it was being written from my grandmother. The postcard was one of the Statue of Liberty with that
well known quote from Emma Lazarus:

> Give me your tired, your poor,
> your huddled masses, yearning to breathe free,
> the wretched refuse of your teeming shore.
> Send these, the homeless, tempest tossed to me.
> I lift my lamp beside the golden door.

Most likely my grandmother was among those tired poor.
She probably felt homeless and tempest tossed on that day in
1899 when she brought my mother here trying to give her the
home she could not provide. On the postcard I began to write:

October 10, 1899/October 10, 1992

Dear Macrina,

A thousand days in God's sight is as yesterday which is
past. October 10, 1899, has been nostalgic in your heart.
You long to be part of it, you ache to know secrets that are
hidden in time, unknown and unknowable. You yearn to
enter into a mystery that was once upon a time, once upon
an October 10. Time is eternal. With God all time is *now!*

I love my daughter, Marion, your mother. Today I have
a sad and difficult journey to make: a journey from 9th
Avenue where she was born, to 68th Street and 3rd Avenue where I pray she will be given a good home.

Learn to trust. Good will come out of my lonely journey,
just as healing will come out of your memorial pilgrimage
to this place. I do what I must do with a heavy and courageous heart. You will some day wish to search out this
mystery. I tell you; let it be. It has already embraced you.

Carry it in your heart remembering that we are ONE. I am
with you always.

Lovingly
Your grandmother,
Annie

I stood up, preparing to leave. My ritual would be complete with the mailing of this card. Then a most amazing oc-
currence took place. Down the street came a young woman
carrying a tiny baby wrapped in a blanket. As she passed me
our eyes met. There was a brief communion, an exchanged
gaze as she continued on. I am not suggesting that this was a
miracle and I was back in time; though it could perhaps be. I
only know that, for me, it was an experience of grace. Something happened in me at that moment. I felt connected to my
past and the amazing truth dawned on me that if my grandmother had not left my mother at the foundling home that day
in 1899, I wouldn't be living today.

Earlier in the week I had made a visit to the address giv-
en to me as my mother's birthplace. The address given to me
was 337 9th Avenue, and that site was now a post office. It was
to this post office on 9th Avenue that I journeyed to mail my
postcard.

Receiving the postcard when I returned home was a special moment for me. I held it as one would hold a prayer, reflecting on my experience of trying to get in touch with my
roots. The circle seemed complete when I answered my grandmother's postcard with this letter.

Dear Grandmother,
During my recent pilgrimage to New York City I had a
precious awakening. The miracle of connections washed
over me. I began to realize that if you had not made your
lonely journey to the Foundling Home on October 10,
1899, I would not be alive today. All the things that led to
my birth would not have taken place. My mother would
not have traveled to Arkansas on the Orphan Train as she

did in 1902. I would never have known the beautiful grandmother who adopted her. She would not have met my father, and so, I simply wouldn't be.

These sacred connections have profoundly moved me and I thank you for the gift of my life. The mystery of my mother's roots has always haunted me. I do not like "the unknown." All I can say now is that I feel a lovely oneness with you. I used to take delight in the fact that even though I never knew you, I was able to gaze at the same moon that you once looked at. Somehow that was a comforting thought, an important bond. My other connection is my mother's name, Marion. Since you gave her that name, it feels like a gift from you. It's the only word that I know for certain that you spoke, "Marion." Sometimes I use Mom's name as a prayer and it seems that you are praying through me. I have no doubt that all things are as they should be.

> I feel safely lost in this mystery,
> Your granddaughter,
> Macrina

When I mailed this letter to the post office on 9th Avenue in New York City with no return address, I realized it would probably be laid to rest in the dead letter office. Somehow that didn't matter. I know my grandmother received it. These simple rituals surrounding the mystery of my roots led me into luminous places. I am at peace with the wonder of the unknown.

REQUIEM FOR A TREE

Once during a summer retreat at our retreat center in Fort Smith a storm came. Lightning! Rolling thunder! Powerful winds! Torrential rains! All the things we associate with storms were present. It was an interesting time for a storm to arrive; we had been praying with the storms of our lives. I had reminded retreatants that lightning puts nitrogen into the soil and I asked them to reflect on what kind of blessings the storms in their lives had brought to them.

The morning after the storm we discovered that a giant oak tree out in front of the center had fallen. It's lovely broken body seemed to cry out for a ritual—a requiem for a fallen tree. The community of retreatants gathered outside. I asked that they form a circle around the tree. For about five minutes we simply stood in silence. We stood in solidarity with everyone who seems to fall before their time. We called out names of individuals and groups of people, cultures, religions, organizations that had remained faithful and true to their ideals in spite of the storms waged against them. An old Quaker hymn came to mind and we sang it as a reminder of the tremendous strength and courage in so many lives.

> No storm can shake my inmost calm
> When to that rock I'm clinging.
> Since love is Lord of heaven and earth,
> How can I keep from singing?

I invited the retreatants to approach the tree and receive a last gift from it. The reverence with which people came forward reminded me of a communion service. Lovingly fingering the broken body of this fallen tree, they took with them pieces of bark, leaves, small branches, acorns. . . .

I share this story with you to suggest that every event in life can be ritualized. Times of ritual celebration often serve as moments of integration and healing, helping us to connect with both joy and sorrow. Rituals have a way of living on in our memories. This was made clear to me about two years after our tree ceremony.

One day I received a package from someone who had been on that retreat. It was a roughly carved cross wrapped in the following message from a woman named Katie:

> I am sending you a cross in the mail! This cross is my prayer: "Here, God, I can't handle it anymore. Take it, it's yours! This is my heartache and this is my obsession.

This is my despair, my gloom. This is my failure, my contempt, my impatience. This is what I need to know and this is what I cannot bear to know. And this is what I do know! This is what I cannot take any longer."

One thing about God—She/he is awfully hard to get a hold of, no address, no telephone, no fax machine, no e-mail, nothing, not even voice mail. I cannot reach God, but I can reach you, Macrina. So here is my cross! This is my confusion, my weariness, my heavy heart. This is my angst, my divorce, my tormented relationships. This is my brother's illness, my sister-in-law's neurotic and cruel behavior, and my bitterness and intolerance that follow. This is my spirit to give up. My death wish. My torture. This is my pain, my sorrow, my grief. This is my long road. My loneliness. Can you do anything with it?

Actually, this is a cross carved from the wood that was taken from the tree which the storm caught at St. Scholastica on my retreat two years ago. Do you remember? We took a small piece of the splintered oak on the day we had our tree ceremony, and recalling the story you told us about the cross and your own healing, I asked Jon to make you this. It was his idea to leave it rugged to symbolize our incompleteness.

It is my way of ritualizing what is going on in my life. I am not totally devoid of hope. Putting my sorrows into this cross has been therapeutic for me. In some way or another sooner or later, we are all struck by lightening, broken like the stately limbs of a beautiful old oak. I have never forgotten the solidarity I felt with the pain of the universe, on the day we had our tree ceremony. That retreat was such a good experience for me.

This is comforting news. Two years after the retreat, a participant is still benefiting from the experience of standing with other seekers around a symbol of brokenness, a fallen tree. Katie is at a much better place in her life today. Having learned something of the peace that comes from forgiving one-self, she is finding her way to the gold in her memories.

HEALING WATERS

Pure, clean, sparkling water. Surely water is one of our healthiest drinks. It's easy to forget, in our great thirst, as we gulp down this precious gift that some people don't have pure water. Some water has to be boiled in order to be safe for drinking. Some people have to walk great distances to get the water that they need. As we allow ourselves to remember this, it can make us more grateful.

Slowly drinking a glass of water can be a kind of ritual. It is our presence, our quiet involvement, in an event that can change it from a commonplace action to a sacred ritual. I discovered this in a rather intimate way in the week before my surgery (which I described in Chapter 2).

On the Notre Dame campus there is a shrine of Our Lady of Lourdes. There is a water fountain at the shrine and the source of the water is a natural spring. During my week of unknowing, that time of uncertainty about my health, I found myself spending a lot of time at the grotto. The water fountain became my healing waters. In my journal I wrote:

At the grotto I have drained the water fountain, drinking in hope that all shall be well. If anyone is keeping tabs on my presence at the grotto they may be inclined to think I'm pious. Not so. I am spending too much time at the grotto, but I am learning something here. I am learning what it is that makes a shrine holy. It is the feet of the pilgrims. How many people pass by, for just a moment they gaze silently. They say a prayer. They light a candle. Drink the water! Stand in silence! Pray the rosary! Kneel in simplicity and abandonment!

It is especially touching to come in the early morning when it is still dark. My first morning drink is from the fountain instead of the coffee pot. That's quite a switch for a coffee lover. There are few people present, often no

one. It looks like a cave of lights—a cave full of prayers—
cries from so many hearts. It is the sorrows and joys,
hopes and despairs, the deep faith that make this place
holy. I am blessed to be here.

The Sacrament of a Candle Flame

How many candles have you lit in your lifetime? And
what is the difference in merely lighting a candle and in allowing that lighted candle to become a prayer? I think you know
the answer to my question. Again, it has something to do with
the quality of your presence. Are you there in the lighting? Are
you there in the burning? Are you present in your longing? The
magic of lighting a candle and praying for something or someone probably resides more in the love present in your heart
than in anything else. We may tend to think that God does
something special when we pray with a lighted candle. It is
probably truer that the lighting of the candle becomes a liturgy
because of our attitude and the faith in our hearts. Magic happens when we learn to be hospitable to life-events rather than
closing them out. Notes from my journal read:

> I have not yet lit a candle. I took a candle early in the
> week. I felt a bit like a thief carrying it away from the
> grotto unlit. I want to fill it with prayer before lighting it.
> It sits unlit in my room. I finger it lovingly, talking to it
> like a god. Why am I doing this? On the morning I leave
> I shall go to the grotto and light it. I'll leave the cry of my
> heart in this holy cave along with all those other cries.

Very early in the morning on the day I left Notre Dame I
wrote:

> I brought my candle to the grotto early this morning. No
> one was there. I placed it in a significant spot in the top
> row. This burning candle is a celebration of my belief in
> and love of life. I am asking that all shall be well, not just
> for myself, but for everyone who cries out for God, for

everyone who prays, and for everyone who would pray if they could but find the heart to do so. This candle is filled with hope and gratitude. That is my prayer. I pray mostly without words. I enter into the mystery of life. My love is my prayer. I have really not asked for anything specific. When you pray for specifics it is so easy to say that God hasn't answered your prayer, but when you lean into the mystery of life and death, of hope, and despair, love and fear, anxiety and peace, of God—how could your prayer be anything but answered. How could you not become a living prayer? When we give up our agenda, we become our prayer.

A half hour before leaving for the airport to come back home from Notre Dame I wrote:

It is raining lightly. I came one last time to look at my candle. In the cave of lights I spoke my doctor's name out loud. Then the strangest thing happened. The basilica bells began to toll. I suppose one of the Holy Cross Fathers died and they were having a funeral. Standing there I was fully aware that some sort of tumor was growing inside me that could be life-threatening. It was not a good time for me to hear the bells toll. For just a moment fear visited me again, but then almost instantaneously peace welled up in me and I thought, "These bells are tolling for this man's life." I stepped back a little from the shrine. The rain was still lightly falling, the sound of the rain on my umbrella and the toll of the bells kind of blended together like a prayer. Each toll I received as a mantra of life, and with each toll I breathed in and out everything I was feeling: courage, hope, fear, love, anxiety, joy, sorrow, peace, potential, harmony, loving kindness, tension, uncertainty, gratitude, death, life. I want to companion everything I feel.

No feeling is unacceptable. But this I know from experience: hope will always be out front for me.

These are some of the ways I have dealt with fear and anxiety in my life. It is really quite amazing how things like lighting a candle, a slow drink of water, a visit to a holy place, standing in silent attention, inviting the raindrops to be prayer, such simple little things can be sacred rituals celebrating our faith and hope in a God who is an intimate part of our life.

Under the Sycamore Trees

Oh, for the days of my youth when I could gather rituals right out of my soul. Ideas leapt out of me like dancing fountains. I miss those day. I've grown too old. Thoughts of doing things correctly crowd out my creativity. I would like to become, once again, a natural celebrant in the cosmic cathedral of the universe. This was my vocation as a child.

We are so much more creative than we remember. We have forgotten about the spontaneous liturgies, that once flowed out of magical springs within, rituals as natural as the quaking of the aspen trees.

Recently a bit of my spontaneity returned. A ritual emerged without any planning. I was spending a few days in a hermitage at our community House of Prayer. The hermitages are located at the founding site of our original monastery. I was fortunate to be there on Founder's Day, January 23. On that day I woke up before dawn. The night before I had been reading some of the history of our founding sisters. I was particularly touched by this quote,

> Even the appearance of their new home was indicative of the poverty and loneliness that was to be so much a part of the founding of the new community. For there, completely surrounded by the woods, stood the small split log convent with the church nearby. Upon entering the sisters' house, Father Wolfgang devoutly prayed, "Peace be to this house," and the sisters responded,

"and to all who dwell herein." Later Sister Bonaventura dryly commented: "I shall tell Mother Agatha that we filled the house with Benedictine peace." Her remark was apt, for that was all that did fill the house for it was completely unfurnished. . . .[5]

Awakening with these thoughts on my mind I desired to spend the day in communion with our pioneer sisters. I decided to fast from sunrise to sunset in memory of those difficult beginning years. My desire to fast had little to do with thoughts of penance. It was more of a desire to enhance my character through a ritual action that would remind me of my true hungers. And it was a pilgrimage to the spirits of our founding sisters. It was a journey in my spirit to their courage, their deep faith and love, their sorrows and joys. I wanted to engage in the prayer of deep remembrance and to bond with those brave women who are part of my history.

Suddenly it became important for me to begin this day out under the sycamore trees. Two trees stand as sentinels near the original monastery site. This site is one of the holy lands of my life. Bundling up for the nippy January weather I carried with me a little candle, a hunk of bread, and an old blanket. I was soon settled out under the stars, on my blanket and under the sycamore trees.

Lighting the candle, I held it in memory of our pioneer sisters who were like lights in the darkness of their new beginnings. On January 23, 1879, as they broke open this land, it was truly a breaking open of the Word of God. After about five minutes I blew out the candle and began waiting patiently for the dawn. Facing the east like a wordless prayer, I waited. As the sun rose above the blue hills I held up the bread, my offering of the day. I broke the bread in three pieces, honoring the lives of our sisters whose lives were broken in so many ways. One piece I received as food for my day's journey. Crumbling up a second piece, I scattered the crumbs under the sycamore trees. I don't really know why I did this. It just happened. The meaning unfolded as the day wore on. We are bread for the world. Our lives must be broken and given as the life of Jesus was broken and given for all. Our sisters enacted this so well in their lives. The scattering of the crumbs represented the sowing of their lives.

The rest of the day was spent in quiet seeing. I walked those holy grounds in memory. I fasted from words and food. No reading! No writing! Only seeing. Walking. Sitting. Gazing. Loving. At sunset I ate my last piece of bread. I will always remember the day that began under the sycamore trees.

Daily Rituals

Many of us have natural rituals that are just automatically built into our day. These rituals are ways of beginning the day, or perhaps, ending the day. Maybe you even have "coming home from work" rituals.

I live in community and have never ceased to be both amazed and amused at the great variety of morning rituals that take place at the sink: brushing of teeth, flossing, gargling, washing one's face, brushing or combing hair, et cetera. If you think there is only one way of doing these little morning rites, look around you and be prepared for a vast display of creativity.

There was once a sister in our community who spent so much time at the sink in the morning that, for a brief period of time, I began worrying that I was somehow missing something essential. As for me, I would come in for my quick-stop: brush my teeth, splash cold water in my face (my way of waking up), toss my head a bit (my way of combing hair), and be on my way for other rituals. Meanwhile the *sister at the sink* labored on. Oh well! We are all unique and that in itself is delightful if we can but remember and cherish the differences.

My morning rituals have more to do with waking the soul. My body awakens rather quickly once I'm out of bed, and it urges me to get moving. But there seems to be another part of me that doesn't want to move at all. That part wants to linger: to consciously receive the new day, to remember who I am, to dwell in the Beloved for a few moments, to be filled with blessings, to wait for the sunrise, to remember people who might need healing on this day. All of these desires have a way of becoming little morning rituals for me.

On most days I spend a few moments grounding myself. This consists of standing in silence at my east window. It is merely a moment of gratitude for who I am, for my health, my talents, my friends, the challenges of the new day.

I often pray to be grounded in the peace that Jesus offered as his parting gift to us. Recently a friend taught me a chant that has become a way of calling in the peace, remembering the peace that resides in us even in the midst of turmoil. For me it is a way of remembering to be peaceful. Using the appropriate gestures I chant, "All before me peaceful, all behind me peaceful, all above me peaceful, all below me peaceful, all around me peaceful, all within me peaceful."

You may wish to use these words as a way of calling in the peace. Make up your own chant or even your own words. Do you remember how as children we used to do this? Children are full of natural melodies that just flow out spontaneously. They don't worry about doing things right or sounding right. Most of us still have a lot of that spontaneity stored in our souls if we can only learn to believe in it.

My morning rituals are no more important than the rituals of the sister who spent such a long time at the sink. This may have been her way of renewing herself for the day. I observed that she did her work cheerfully and was concerned about others, especially the sick. Perhaps her great awakening took place at the sink. And what about you? How do you awaken to the new day?

The gold in my life often gets lost in the cracks of my busyness. I frequently design rituals to help me harvest the beauty of the present moment. For example, upon receiving a letter from a friend, rather than ripping it open and reading it while walking back to my office, I might put it aside for awhile. Then, later when I take a coffee break, I can sit down and read the letter with so much more presence than would have been possible had I read it while hurriedly rushing back to my work. These may seem like unimportant items, but they serve as a means of calling us to attention. Thus, they are pathways to finding the gold.

FIRE RITUAL

For those of us who are journalers, there comes a day when we have to decide just how many of our words are worth saving. Shelves full of journals make me nervous after awhile, and more than ever since I've had my words published.

Two of my most memorable ritual events took place at a fire pit. The first occurred about five years after my final profession as a monastic. It was the day I decided to burn all my novitiate journals. During a retreat I reread most of my journals, shed some tears, laughed a lot, and found myself saying, "Oh my, I've grown a lot since those days." I wrote down some notes in my new journal and then made a trip to the barbecue pit behind the tennis courts. The burning was a prayer in living color.

Amazingly, it was quite easy. I think I was more detached in those days. I tore up the pages and gave them to the flames. In so doing I believed I was giving those years of my life to God. The journals were written in the tone of a young person longing to learn how to love God and others. I decided then and there that I didn't need to save the words in the journals. What I needed to save was that intense yearning for God.

My second and more recent pilgrimage to the fire pit was actually a lot more difficult. I have lost some of the fervor of those post-novitiate days, and so perhaps I had grown more attached to the journals I was burning. However, what motivated me to let them go was my reading of Thomas Merton's personal journals. I have always loved Merton, and I love reading his new journals. In his journals, though, I was surprised to come upon names of people I knew personally, and suddenly I thought, "What if I should die and someone would try to publish my journals?"

I realize this was not a thought full of trust and abandonment to divine providence. The thought was probably filled more with grandiosity than humility; still this reverie set me on edge. It also startled me into reflecting on my words, both written and spoken. There seem to be too many around for my own good, and I buy into them all too easily. I'm always looking for another book to read, another word to give me life. If I could just sit with the Word instead of reading, writing, and speaking so many words, I'd be better off. If those who read my books would spend that time in quiet wordless centering they would probably be better off too.

And still I write. Why? What is this in me that longs for solitude, yet pours out so many words? I think it has something to do with that same intense yearning for God that I found in my old novitiate journals. I am glad to know the yearning is still alive and well.

With that same gladness in my heart I gave my words to God. I let the flames consume them, but it was not easy. It was hard to let them go. I felt as though I was burning my prayer book. Once in awhile I even find myself missing them, but for the most part I am glad for the fire and pray that it continues to consume in me whatever is not for God's glory.

The experience of burning my journals was a ritual. It was my attempt to remember who I am, to remember who I was, and to remember the person I want to be. It was a prayer.

Holiday Rituals

Can you remember rituals that took place in your childhood home? Try to recall endearing patterns or ways of living life together in your family. Two memories that are uniquely precious to me are connected to the celebration of Christmas and Easter.

On Christmas Eve we gathered in the kitchen to wait for the arrival of Santa. We would often have popcorn or some kind of treat while we were waiting. It was one time we were never told to be quiet. It seems that noise was essential, for in the next room Santa was putting out gifts, and we weren't supposed to know that he was in there at that moment. After awhile, Mama would say, "Let's turn out the lights and sit here and wait in the darkness." Although we were waiting for

Christmas, which to us meant bright lights, candy, surprises, little gifts, it was always explained to us that we were waiting for Christ. In the darkness of the kitchen we could see the light in the next room. We knew that when the light went out that meant that Santa was finished and we were free to go in.

Going into that room was a ritual I will never forget. It is such a dear memory in my life especially because I now realize that my parents had little money to buy gifts, yet the magical moment of entering that room is forever etched in my heart. All was in darkness. We were each given a sparkler. We went into the Christmas tree room in silence. Our sparklers were lit. The Christmas tree lights were turned on. Christ was born again in the joy of that moment.

I'm somewhat in awe of my parents' creativity. This lovely ritual of waiting in the darkness and then everything bursting into light is the best Christmas gift I've ever received. It spoke of the *past*: a people waiting in the darkness. It said much about who we were at this *present* moment: children able to receive joy and love, capable of being delighted by simple, inexpensive gifts. It revealed loving parents who, even in their great poverty, found ways of making Christmas special. And now as I look back I can see how in many ways, it pointed to the *future*: our lives were being shaped by this lovely ritual. This moment in time would linger in our hearts. The memory of celebrating Christ in our home would enrich our faith life. As I ponder this now, still touched by the memory, I can see endless ways that the ritual we celebrated on those Christmas evenings so long ago still has the power to delight me.

Of course, innocence doesn't last forever. I soon learned words like *more* and *less*. Eventually those words got in the way of my original simple joy of receiving. I started comparing my gifts with the gifts of others. And yet, I am grateful for that magical moment of waiting in the darkness for Christmas. That festive family ritual lives on in my life as a golden memory.

Easter is another one of my bright memories. There are times when I have been slightly embarrassed that I could have ever believed anything so ridiculous as a rabbit coming around and laying colored eggs. However, I was a devout disciple of the Easter Bunny. My mother had a clever way of getting us out of the house when she wanted to color the eggs. We were sent out to the woods and meadows to gather flowers and grasses to make our Easter nests. She would always tell us she had work to do, so we knew she wanted us to be gone for awhile. We were to play, and enjoy the woods, and take our time. We were not to disturb her. It was a great outing.

When we arrived back at the house with our sacks full of treasures we would each find a choice place under a spirea bush or in the flower garden where we would create our nests. Then Mama would come out of the house with a plate of cookies for a treat. With great excitement we would show her our artistically designed nests. On Easter morning we would rush out to discover those nests filled with bright colored eggs and sometimes little chocolate bunnies and chicks.

Do you remember any family rituals designed to help you celebrate special feast days? Talk about them with others. Exchange ideas. Try out your own creativity in developing new holiday rituals.

FAMILY REUNIONS

The word "reunion" suggests a *gathering together* of what has become scattered. It is a friendly gathering, a bringing in the kin. Of course, the ones who are kin to us may not necessarily be kindred spirits. We have no choice in being related to one another; we do have a choice as to whether we want to remain or become kindred spirits. A kindred spirit relationship requires that we be willing to take the time to create and nurture a sustaining bond with each other. Our frenetic schedules often make abiding relationships difficult. It is quite a challenge for families to become and remain kindred spirits to one another. Then, too, we have our past histories of living together. We often meet with old pains and resentments stashed away. We come to the reunion and we leave our forgiveness at home.

In spite of all this, family reunions hold wonderful possibilities. My vision of an ideal family reunion is a gathering during which a marvelous rekindling takes place. Bonds are renewed. Old wounds are remembered and talked about. In the midst of tears and laughter, stories are shared. In the telling of stories we lead one another to the golden memories. And we pray together. Yes, there must be prayer. Prayer is communion. We find ways to be in communion with each other and with our God. Prayer can bring about a rekindling of the heart.

I have happy dreams of this great rekindling becoming a reality in my life. I would like to see it become a reality for you also. With this in mind, and for our mutual encouragement, I have created a "rekindling service" to be used at family reunions.

In designing this service I have in mind a reunion for first and second generations. Although I am sharing some ideas about this rekindling service for family reunions, I encourage you to improvise, add or subtract from my format. You know your family and what might work best for them. Make the changes that you need so that this becomes a ritual you can comfortably celebrate with one another.

You will need a large family candle and two different sizes of taper candles. The larger tapers represent the first generation children. The smaller tapers represent the various households of succeeding generations.

The large candle will be your ancestral candle. It is to symbolize the lives of your parents, grandparents, etc. You may wish to make your own candle or purchase a candle. If you make your candle I suggest you put in various colors of wax to signify the siblings in your first generation family. If you purchase the candle you can add the colors to the candle by using paints. Since each color is to represent one person of the first generation family, the colored tapers can be purchased accordingly.

For example: Let's say you come from a family of four children. Your ancestral candle should contain a color for each of these children, e.g., blue, green, purple, red. If blue represents the oldest child, then his or her taper and the taper for all his or her descendants will be blue.

Family members who plan this ceremony may wish to make a small clay candle holder for each taper. On the evening of the gathering, taper candles are arranged around the large family candle. The ceremony begins with the blessing and lighting of the family candle. An appropriate opening song may be chosen. With the help of these introductory remarks you will be able to lead and adapt for your own purposes the candle lighting ritual given here.

A Rekindling Service

Opening song (if desired)
Oldest member of family holds candle. All stand.

Blessing and Lighting of the Ancestral Candle
God of our History, Keeper of our stories, Dreamer of our dreams, this candle represents the lives of (*name first-generation parents*) and all their ancestors and descendants. With you there is no time. One day is like a thousand years. O Ancient Love, support us as we attempt to reach back into our history. Bond us with the mothers and fathers of our past. Rekindle in our lives the faith, hope, and love of our parents, grandparents, great-grandparents, and all our unknown ancestors. Gather into your sacred heart any chapter in our history that needs mending. Healer of hearts, integrate the joys and sorrows of our ancestry that we may experience healing.

With all the love that is in our hearts we bless this candle (*raise hands in gesture of blessing*) and we light it in honor of our family's ancestors. (*light candle*) In the lighting of this candle may our hearts be filled with love and peace. May this light remind us of the flame of courage and faith that burned in the hearts of our ancestors in the midst of the many hardships and uncertainties of their lives. May this candle also burn for the joys and successes of their lives.

In Christ's name we pray. Amen.

Enthronement of the Candle

The candle is now reverently placed in a special place that has been prepared for it. You may wish to decorate this area with flowers, photographs, or special reminders of your first-generation parents.

Siblings (and their spouses, if applicable) of first-generation parents now receive their tapers and light them from the Family Candle. After receiving the light they move to assigned places in the room.

Second-generation members come forward to receive their tapers. Upon receiving their candles each person goes to his or her parents to receive the light from their candle. (Spouses or partners are always included.)

If third-generation members are present, repeat this process.

The large ancestral candle is now placed in the center of the room. The various family groups cluster around this candle.

The children present are now invited to gather in the center around the ancestral candle.

Blessing of the Children

(As the blessing prayer is said, you may wish to invite the family members to raise their hands in a gesture of blessing.)

Source of all life, thank you for the life-gift of the children gathered in this family circle.

We remember the invitation of Jesus, "Let the children come to me, and do not hinder them." And so we invite them. May the openness and innocence of these children be a blessing that follows them through life. May they be healthy. May they grow in wisdom and grace. May they always walk with God. May they learn to love. May these children and their descendants bring forth into their world all that is good, all that is beautiful, all that is true.

If there is anything in our family history that is keeping us stuck in harmful patterns or addictions, may these children and their descendants be the ones who break out of bondage moving into freedom. May they rekindle the light in our hearts that sometimes grows dim. May the light of Christ lead them. Amen.

Turn out lights. All stand in silence for a few moments receiving the love and energy and light that pervades the sacred space this room has become.

A chant or song would be appropriate here.

Another suggestion is a litany of family members who have died. As the names of past ancestors are called out, all reverently reply Pray for us.

Closing Prayer

Spirit of the Living God, look upon this family gathered in the name of Jesus. Rekindle our spirits. Create in us hearts open to each other. Renew the bond of family ties.

Reconcile our lives. May we feel secure in the embrace of your love. Help us not to turn away from past hurts in our family that harm our relationships one to the other. Free the forgiveness in us that waits to be given. Encourage us to pray for each other when we are apart. Gather us in your heart. Be our Kindred Spirit and teach us how to rekindle our love for one another.

Embraced in Christ, we pray. Amen.

It is my hope that this ritual for a family reunion might serve to assist you and your family to call home some of the golden memories, to create new memories, and to allow healing to enter into the broken places of your lives. If we take the time to check the files of our hearts we will discover that they are full of stories. These stories need to be saved. We save them by telling them to one another. It is always a bit amazing to me how, when stories are told, there are many versions of the same story. This doesn't necessarily mean that one person's memory is more accurate than another's. Each of us remembers the story in a unique way. Each person's version is important. Together we create the mosaic of our family history.

Gathering together to remember our lives can be a liturgical moment, a sacred ritual. The word *reunion* means to reunite, to connect, to restore. We renew the bonds we once experienced and still would share if our lives were less complicated, if distance, time, and space wouldn't keep us apart.

God's dream for you is reunion and integration. In what ways do you need to gather up who you really are? Are you willing to explore the recesses of your soul? You may be surprised to discover many treasures waiting in the holy darkness of your life.

What are their names? Abandoned dreams. Forgotten beauty. Hidden sorrows. Hidden joys. Unused energies. Unknown strengths. Lost ages. Undiscovered gifts. Unsung songs. Neglected relationships. Unclaimed wisdom. Cautious love. Unattended anger. Imprisoned forgiveness. Hesitant prayers. Homeless feelings. Timid truth. Buried stories. Lost memories. All these are veins of gold waiting to be mined.

EXERCISES

1. Are there some natural rituals that have become a part of your life, sacred patterns and ways of doing things? Take time to reflect on this and then list them in your journal.

2. What family rituals do you remember from your childhood? Write a letter to one of your ancestors describing the gold in your memories.

3. Create a ritual of thanksgiving to close your day. When you become comfortable with this ritual, invite someone to share it with you.

4. Who are the kindred spirits in your life?

5. At times it can be helpful to pray with something that is touchable, something you can pick up and hold and use throughout the day. Praying with tangible objects can assist you in discovering your own creativity. Gather up the following articles: a Band-Aid, an old pair of glasses, a

photograph, an old letter, a spool of thread, a candle that is almost used up, a dry twig from a tree. You may wish to replace some of these things with your own choices. Choose one of these objects for each of the next seven days. Create your morning prayer around it. Share this experience with someone.

6. Now that you have prayed with these tangible items, I encourage you to find a copy of Joyce Rupp's delightful book *The Cup of Our Life* (Ave Maria Press, 1997). She asks you to pray with a cup. This book is full of wonderful suggestions for your prayer, and it is a great source for introducing you to simple daily rituals.

7. Prayerfully review and share the gold in your memories with family members.

Conclusion

*Take care
and be earnestly on your guard
not to forget
the things which your eyes have seen,
nor let them slip from your memory
as long as you live,
. . . teach them to your children
and to your children's children.*

— Deuteronomy 4:9

Echoes from the past resound through our beings. Shadows of memories enfold us. Transient, subtle, shy, and fleeting! How easy it is for things to slip from our memories. We sometimes forget God's mercies and promises. We forget our own goodness, our love and our compassion. The stories that have made us who we are, our family history—they all slip away from us. Wonderful as memories can be, they are also elusive. And so, we have to practice remembering. It takes a lot of care to assure that these stories do not slip away into oblivion.

Before closing this book it might be helpful to ask yourself a few questions:

❧ What stories from your family history need to be written down and passed on?

❧ What memories in your life need to be saved?

❧ How can you touch again memories that appear to be lost?

❧ How can you offer hospitality even to painful memories?

❧ Do you need a counselor to walk through some memories with you?

❧ Are there some memories that should be left alone?

❧ How can you make new memories?

❧ What is your dearest memory of God?

❧ Have you considered the importance of solitude on your quest of remembering?

I often say to parents: Tell your children stories from the past. Likewise I remind young people: Ask your parents and grandparents questions about your ancestry. Beg them for stories—family rituals and episodes, events and experiences, memories of aunts and uncles, cousins, neighbors. Ask before it's too late. Ask before the ones who hold the stories have passed to another shore.

As John O'Donohue so correctly points out, our technological age has belittled the concept of memory: "To say that computers have memory is false. A computer has storage and

recall. Human memory is, however, more refined, sacred, and personal."[1]

Let us go, then, to the place where the past has gathered—the house of memory. O'Donohue calls this place a temple. Frederick Buechner names it a Room Called Remember. Jesus says he is going away to prepare a dwelling place for us, a place where we will remember and be remembered by God. It seems fitting that this place of memories be called a temple, or even a tabernacle. Memory is the ground of our identity. Out of the soil of the past, green shoots reach up toward the future.

Take care to spend time in your temple of memory. "O God, we ponder your love within your temple," the psalmist prays (Psalm 48:10). Within the temple of ourselves, we, too, ponder the joys and sorrows of our lives. They are part of God's glory in us. The seeds of memory contain a spiritual energy that can help to shape our future.

But how should we approach this temple when not all of the memories that await us are pleasant? Perhaps we can approach it as Moses approached the burning bush, filled with memories from his past. Yes, let us come with trembling and awe! With bare feet and open hearts! With a willingness to be hospitable to all memories so that the past, present, and future might experience a kinship. Take off your shoes; the ground you stand on is holy. Approach the temple of yourself with reverent awe and a willingness to wait for revelation.

Do not, then, tug at your memories like children trying to hasten the opening of a bud. Life's revelations always involve a dying. Out of that dying comes new life. C. S. Lewis says it like this:

> Properly bedded down in a past we do not miserably try to conjure back, memories will send up exquisite growths. Leave the bulbs alone, and the new flowers will come up. Grub them up, and hope, by fondling and sniffling, to get last year's blooms, and you will get nothing. "Unless the seed die."[2]

A quiet presence in our house of memories is necessary in order for us to make the life-giving connections that will bring us awareness and wisdom. This is why I recommend a certain amount of solitude, that we may be able to offer our memories the kind of hospitality they need. For those of us who are willing to wait, symbols will be given to assist us in remembering.

In the book *Stones From the River*, we meet a captivating and endearing character named Trudi. Trudi is a dwarf. Thus, she has experienced the pain and loneliness that comes with being different from others. At one point in the story she goes to the village doctor asking for a pill that will help her grow. In telling this story she says that a look of pain crossed the doctor's face as she explained that there was no such pill.

Trudi feels compassion for the doctor's sadness. In her heart of hearts she tries to believe that whatever in her needs to grow is just resting. She believes that if the right thing can be found to trigger the growth, it will happen.[3]

As I listen to Trudi's longing to be able to connect with the *right thing* that will make her grow, I see how this can be applied to our memories. Sometimes just the right symbol can trigger a memory. Then other memories, like new green shoots from hidden roots, will start reaching upward. In order for this to take place, though, we must be willing to keep vigil in the temple of our memories.

One of the best ways for me to get in touch with my memories is through solitude and writing. You have probably noticed that I designed this book with that in mind. I invite you to spend time in solitude and I encourage you to write. Pick up your pen and write. Write about the colors and sounds, the smells and sights of this day. Describe the people who have passed through your life this week. As you give voice to your present memories you will gradually be able to take a few steps back into your past and awaken other memories.

In her creative writing classes Anne Lamott fires her students with a desire to write. Writing, she reminds us, eases our loneliness and reduces our feelings of separation. As we write, she claims,

We are given a shot at dancing with, or at least clapping along with the absurdity of life, instead of being squashed by it over and over again. It's like singing on a boat during a terrible storm at sea. You can't stop the raging storm, but singing can change the hearts and spirits of the people who are together on that ship.[4]

These lines hint at a spiritual energy that abides in each of us. As we learn to tap into this energy, we will be encouraged to dance and sing with all of our memories. Each one of us houses a dynamic power that can lead us into the future filled with hope. This same vibrant power can help us to make new memories rather than staying trapped in memories that burden us. At the end of each day ask yourself, "What new memories have I made this day?"

This morning, for example, while I was sitting in my sister's garden listening to the running water of the garden fountain I saw a hummingbird winging its way in and out of the water. Darting, fluttering, dancing! Showering and drinking on the run—but oh, with such grace! And now, as evening shadows enfold me, I carry with me the eternity of that moment. The dance of the hummingbird lives on in my memory because I was present not only in body, but with my whole heart and soul.

Here is the secret of making new memories. Learn to abide in the present moment. Are you really tasting that first cup of morning coffee? Do you feel the warm cleansing waters flowing over your body as you take a shower, or are you already five miles into your work day? Can you live in the moment? Are you able to be there? Can you recall the faces of those with whom you've shared your day? Do you notice your friend's carefree, windblown look? Did you truly see the person you had lunch with today? Did you notice the anxiety in her voice or the grateful look in his eyes? Do you remember what you ate for lunch? Did you notice the wind blowing through the leaves of the tree outside your window? Were you, perhaps, a good memory in someone's life today simply because of your attentive presence?

Look all around you. Look well! Invite the "poet in residence" in your soul to accompany you through this day. There's a whole world of memories out there waiting to be made. Live well, my friend. Stay well. Remember well. Make new memories. And abide!

Food for the Soul:
An Offering of Books

Here is my gift of reading for you. These are among the books that nourish and bless me. The ones marked with an (*) are memoirs or have a memoir flavor. As you try to get in touch with the gold in your memories, a good book can be like a friend at your side. May you always have good book-friends.

Adams, Ann. *The Silver Boat*. Cincinnati, OH: BSC, Inc. Publications, 1990.

Alan, Thomas B. *Offerings at the Wall*. Atlanta, GA: Turner Publications, 1995.

* Anaya, Rudolfo A. *Bless Me Ultima*. Berkeley, CA: TQS Publications, 1972.

Ayo, Nicholas. *Sacred Marriage: The Wisdom of the Song of Songs*. New York: Continuum, 1997.

Buechner, Frederick. *Listening to Your Life*. San Francisco: HarperSanFrancisco, 1992.

* _____. *Telling Secrets: A Memoir*. San Francisco: Harper SanFrancisco, 1991.

Burnett, Frances Hodgson. *The Secret Garden*. New York: HarperCollins, 1938.

* Butala, Sharon. *The Perfection of the Morning*. Toronto: Harper Perennial, 1994.

* Brown, John Gregory. *Decorations in a Ruined Cemetery*. New York: Avon Books, 1995.

* Carroll, James. *An American Requiem, God, My Father, and the War That Came Between Us*. New York: Houghton Mifflin, 1996.

Chodron, Pema. *Start Where You Are: A Guide to Compassionate Living*. Boston: Shambhala, 1994.

Courtenay, Bryce. *The Power of One*. New York: Ballantine Books, 1991.

* D'Arcy, Paula. *Song for Sarah: A Young Mother's Journey Through Grief and Beyond*. Wheaton, IL: Harold Shaw, 1979.

* _____. *Gift of the Red Bird: A Spiritual Encounter*. New York: Crossroad, 1996.

Dunne, John S. *Love's Mind: An Essay on Contemplative Life*. Notre Dame, IN: University of Notre Dame Press, 1993.

* Estes, Clarissa Pinkola. *The Faithful Gardener.* San Francisco: HarperSanFrancisco, 1995.

Finley, James. *Merton's Palace of Nowhere.* Notre Dame, IN: Ave Maria Press, 1978.

Fox, Mem. *Wilfred Gordon McDonald Patridge.* Brooklyn, New York & La Jolla, CA: Kane/Miller Books, First American Edition 1985. (A lovely children's story about a little boy helping an old woman find her lost memories.)

* Gibbons, Kaye. *Ellen Foster.* New York: Random House, 1987.

Grahame, Kenneth. *The Wind in the Willows.* New York: The New American Library, Inc., 1969.

* Hays, David. *Passion Below Zero: Essays from Last Chance, Idaho.* Ketchum, ID: Lost River Press, 1995.

Hifler, Joyce Sequichie. *A Cherokee Feast of Days.* Tulsa, OK: Council Oak Books, 1992—my favorite daily meditation book.

* Hillisum, Etty. *An Interrupted Life: Diaries of Etty Hillisum.* New York: Washington Square Press, 1981.

* Holtz, Albert, O.S.B. *A Saint on Every Corner.* Notre Dame, IN: Ave Maria Press, 1998.

Howatch, Susan. *Church of England Series* (novels) beginning with *Glittering Images* and ending with *Absolute Truths.* New York: Ballantine Books, 1987-1994.

Irving, John. *A Prayer for Owen Meany.* New York: William Morrow & Co., 1989.

" Johnson, Nancy and Wooldrige, Shirley. *The Secret Gift. Discovering God's Grace.* Austin, TX: John Ridge Press, 1996.

Johnston, William. *The Cloud of Unknowing.* New York: Doubleday, 1973.

Keats, John. *Complete Poetry and Selected Prose of John Keats.* New York: Random House, 1951.

* Kidd, Sue Monk. *The Dance of the Dissident Daughter.* San Francisco: HarperSanFrancisco, 1996.

* Macdougall, Allan Ross, ed. *Letters of Edna St. Vincent Millay.* New York: Grosset & Dunlap, 1952.

Markova, Dawna. *No Enemies Within.* Berkeley, CA: Conari Press, 1994.

Merrill, Nan C. *Psalms for Praying: An Invitation to Wholeness.* New York: Continuum, 1997.

* Merton, Thomas. *The Journals of Thomas Merton Vol. 1-7.* San Francisco: HarperSanFrancisco.

* _____. *The Sign of Jonas.* New York: Harcourt, Brace and Co., 1953.

Mitcham, Marylee. *An Accidental Monk.* Cincinnati, OH: St. Anthony Messenger Press, 1976.

* Noble, Christina with Robert Coram. *Bridge Across My Sorrows.* London: Transworld Publishers Ltd., Corgi Books, 1995.

* Norris, Kathleen. *Dakota.* New York: Tichnor & Fields, 1993.

O'Donohue, John. *Anam Cara: A Book of Celtic Wisdom.* San Francisco: HarperSanFrancisco, 1997.

Oliver, Mary. *New and Selected Poems.* Boston: Beacon Press, 1992.

Paton, Alan. *Too Late the Phalarope.* New York: Scribner, 1953.

_____. *Cry the Beloved Country.* New York: Scribner, 1948.

Rilke, Ranier Maria. *Rilke's Book of Hours: Love Poems to God,* translated by Anita Barrows and Joanna Macy. New York: Riverhead Books, 1996.

Rupp, Joyce. *The Cup of Our Life: A Guide for Spiritual Growth.* Notre Dame, IN: Ave Maria Press, 1997.

* _____. *Dear Heart, Come Home.* New York: Crossroad, 1996.

* Sarton, May. *Journal of a Solitude.* New York: W.W. Norton, 1978.

* Scott, Barbara J. *The Violet Shyness of Their Eyes: Notes From Nepal.* Corvallis: Calyx Books, 1993.

Stendl-Rast, David. *The Music of Silence.* San Francisco: HarperSanFrancisco, 1995.

Strong, Mary, ed. *Letters of the Scattered Brotherhood.* Harper & Row, 1948. (There is a new edition of this book out by HarperSanFrancisco.)

van der Post, Laurens. *A Story Like the Wind.* New York: William Morrow & Co., 1972.

_____. *A Far-Off Place.* New York: William Morrow & Co., 1974.

* _____. *The Lost World of the Kalahari*. New York: William Morrow & Co., 1958.

* _____. *The Heart of the Hunter*. New York: William Morrow & Co., 1961.

* _____. *A Walk With A White Bushman*: van der Post in conversation with Jean-Marc Pottiez. New York: William Morrow & Co., 1986.

* Whiteley, Opal, presented by Benjamin Hoff. *The Singing Creek Where the Willows Grow*. New York: Warner Books, 1986.

Whyte, David. *The Heart Aroused: Poetry and the Preservation of the Soul in Corporate America*. New York: Doubleday, 1994.

_____. *The House of Belonging*. Langley, WA: Many Rivers Press, 1997.

Wiederkehr, Macrina. *The Song of the Seed: A Monastic Way of Tending the Soul*. San Francisco: HarperSanFrancisco, 1995.

* Williams, Terry Tempest. *Refuge*. New York: Vintage Books, 1991.

Wood, Nancy. *Dancing Moons*. New York: Doubleday, 1995.

The following books are guides to creativity and writing. These can be valuable companions for you as you begin to journal with your memories.

Albert, Susan Wittig. *Writing from Life: Telling Your Soul's Story.* New York: G. P. Putnam's Sons, 1996.

Baldwin, Christina. *One to One: Self-Understanding Through Journal Writing.* New York: M. Evans and Company, 1977.

Brown, Rita Mae. *Starting From Scratch: A Different Kind of Writers' Manual.* New York: Bantam Books, 1988.

Cameron, Julia. *The Artist's Way: A Spiritual Path to Higher Creativity.* New York: G. P. Putnam's Sons, 1992.

Fox, John. *Find What You Didn't Lose: Expressing Your Truth and Creativity Through Poem-Making.* New York: G.P. Putnam's Sons, 1995.

Goldberg, Natalie. *Writing Down the Bones.* Boston: Shambhala, 1986.

Hass, Robert, ed. *The Essential Haiku: Versions of Basho, Buson and Issa.* Hopewell, NJ: The Eco Press, 1994.

Lamott, Anne. *Bird by Bird: Some Instructions on Writing and Life.* New York: Pantheon, 1994.

Shaughnessy, Susan. *Walking on Alligators: A Book of Meditations for Writers.* San Francisco: HarperSanFrancisco, 1993.

Strand, Clark. *Seeds from a Birch Tree: Writing Haiku and the Spiritual Journey.* New York: Hyperion, 1997.

Ueland, Brenda. *If You Want to Write: A Book About Art, Independence and Spirit.* St. Paul, MN: Grey Wolf Press, 1987.

Welty, Eudora. *One Writer's Beginning.* Cambridge, MA: Harvard University Press, 1983.

Notes

Introduction

1. "The Beads of Life," from Nancy Wood, *Dancing Moons* (New York: Doubleday, 1995), p. 55.

Chapter 1

1. Frances Hodgson Burnett, *The Secret Garden* (New York, HarperCollins, 1938), p. 296-297.

2. John Keats from "Endymion," *Complete Poetry and Selected Prose of John Keats,* ed. by Harold Edgar Briggs (New York. Random House, 1951), p. 65.

3. Frederick Buechner, *Listening to Your Life* (San Francisco: HarperSanFrancisco, 1992), p. 51.

4. Ann Adams, *The Silver Boat* (Cincinnati, OH: BSC Inc. Publications, 1990).

Chapter 2

1. Rainer Maria Rilke, *Rilke's Book of Hours: Love Poems of God,* translated by Anita Burrows and Joanna Macy (New York, Riverhead Books, 1996), p. 47.

2. Anne Lamott, *Bird by Bird* (New York: Pantheon, 1994), p. 125.

3. William Johnston, *The Cloud of Unknowing* (New York: Doubleday, 1973), pp. 54-55.

Chapter 3

1. Frances Hodgson Burnett, *The Secret Garden* (New York, HarperCollins, 1938), pp. 84-85.

2. Kenneth Grahame, *The Wind in the Willows* (New York: The New American Library, Inc., 1969), pp. 27-30.

3. Clarissa Pinkola Estes, *The Faithful Gardener* (San Francisco: HarperSanFrancisco, 1995), p. 19.

4. Ibid., p. 75.

5. *Letters of the Scattered Brotherhood*, edited by Mary Strong (New York: Harper & Row, 1948), pp. 175-176.

6. Laurens van der Post, *The Heart of the Hunter* (New York: William Morrow & Co., 1961), p. 141.

7. Ibid., p. 138.

8. Dawna Markova, *No Enemies Within* (Berkeley, CA: Conari Press, 1994), p. 64.

9. Pema Chodron, *Start Where You Are: A Guide to Compassionate Living* (Boston: Shambhala, 1994), p. 92.

10. David Hays, from the essay "Home," *Passion Below Zero: Essays from Last Chance, Idaho* (Ketchum, ID: Lost River Press, 1995), pp. 5-6.

11. Quoted in John S. Dunne, *Love's Mind: An Essay on Contemplative Life* (Notre Dame, IN: University of Notre Dame Press, 1993), p. 20.

12. Hays, from the essay "Knowing How," pp. 244-245.

13. Alan Paton, *Cry the Beloved Country* (New York: Scribner, 1953), p. 75.

14. Ibid., p. 108.

15. Alan Paton, *Too Late the Phalarope* (New York: Scribner, 1948), p. 266.

16. Thomas Merton, *The Sign of Jonas* (New York: Harcourt, Brace and Co., 1953), pp. 360-362.

17. Sharon Butala, *The Perfection of the Morning* (Toronto: Harper Perennial, 1994), p. 187.

18. David Stendl-Rast, *The Music of Silence* (San Francisco: HarperSanFrancisco, 1995), pp. 102-103.

19. Susan Howatch, *Church of England Series* (novels) beginning with *Glittering Images* and ending with *Absolute Truths* (New York: Ballantine Books, 1987-1994), pp. 459-460.

20. John Irving, *A Prayer for Owen Meany* (New York, William Morrow & Co., 1989), p. 13.

21. Marylee Mitcham, *An Accidental Monk* (Cincinnati, OH: St. Anthony Messenger Press, 1976), pp. 7-9.

22. Ibid., p. 40.

23. Sue Monk Kidd, *The Dance of the Dissident Daughter* (San Francisco: HarperSanFrancisco, 1996), p. 66.

24. Christina Noble with Robert Coram, *Bridge Across My Sorrows* (London: Transworld Publishers Ltd., Corgi Books, 1995), pp. 306-307.

CHAPTER 4

1. Estes, p. 75.

2. John O'Donohue, *Anam Cara: A Book of Celtic Wisdom* (San Francisco: HarperSanFrancisco, 1997), p. 178.

3. Macrina Wiederkehr, *The Song of the Seed: A Monastic Way of Tending the Soul* (San Francisco: HarperSanFrancisco, 1995), p. 115-116.

4. Thomas B. Alan, *Offerings at the Wall* (Atlanta, GA: Turner Publications, 1995).

5. Louise Sharum, OSB, *Write the Vision Down* (Fort Smith: St. Scholastica Monastery, 1979), p. 8.

CONCLUSION

1. O'Donohue, p. 173.

2. C. S. Lewis, *The Joyful Christian* (New York: Macmillan, 1970), p. 79.

3. Ursula Hegi, *Stones From the River* (New York: Scribner, 1994), pp. 53-54.

4. Lamott, p. 237.

Photo by Judith Brower, O.S.B.

Macrina Wiederkehr, O.S.B. is a Benedictine Sister at St. Scholastica Center in Fort Smith, Arkansas. She travels widely to offer retreats and conferences and is the author of three previous books: *A Tree Full of Angels, Seasons of Your Heart,* and *The Song of the Seed* (all from HarperSan Francisco).